To Alejandro and Milly,

This is from our friend Jane Rumph. It is fun reading. We were in the same Sunday school class in Passdena, CA.

We love you two! Keep pressing in, to know Jesus.
Grace and peace,

SIGNS AND WONDERS IN AMERICA TODAY

Mike & Jenny Thorne

Travel

Signs and Wonders in America Today

Amazing Accounts of God's Power

JANE RUMPH

SERVANT PUBLICATIONS
Ann Arbor, Michigan

Vine Books is an imprint of Servant Publications especially designed to serve evangelical Christians.

Servant Publications—Mission Statement

We are dedicated to publishing books that spread the gospel of Jesus Christ, help Christians to live in accordance with that gospel, promote renewal in the church, and bear witness to Christian unity.

Published by Servant Publications
P.O. Box 8617
Ann Arbor, Michigan 48107
www.servantpub.com

Cover design by PAZ Design Group, Salem, Oreg.

03 04 05 06 10 9 8 7 6 5 4 3 2 1

Printed in the United States of America
ISBN 1-56955-296-7

Library of Congress Cataloging-in-Publication Data

Rumph, Jane, 1957-
   Signs and wonders in America today : amazing accounts of God's power /
Jane Rumph.
      p. cm.
   ISBN 1-56955-296-7 (alk. paper)
   1. Miracles. 2. Spiritual healing--United States. I. Title.
   BT97.3.R86 2003
   231.7'3--dc21

2002156460

Contents

ONE

This Could Be the Start of Something Big

BRENDA BEAS GLANCED at my husband with a gleam in her eye. "What do you think?" she asked. "Shall we try doing a 'Peter Wagner'?"

Dave Rumph knew exactly what she meant. They were about to pray for someone's short leg to grow.

My husband, Dave, now serves as president of the 120 Fellowship, an adult class at Lake Avenue Church in Pasadena, California. C. Peter Wagner founded the class (named for the 120 believers of Acts 1:15) in 1982, while a professor at Fuller Seminary's School of World Mission. His research and teaching on signs and wonders, strategic prayer ministry, and other cutting-edge topics shaped and guided the 120 Fellowship in distinctive ways. Peter himself has received a special gift from God to pray for healing of backs and skeletal conditions. Countless times the class has watched as Peter prayed for others, and we have learned to minister similarly.

However, Peter and his wife, Doris, moved to Colorado Springs in 1996 after starting Global Harvest Ministries, on whose board of directors Dave and I serve. For a time many wondered if 120 Fellowship would continue. After a transition we came to see that God still had plans for the class in both pastoral care and ministry areas, although we shrank to more of an extended family size. The healing prayer team joined the larger church's growing prayer ministry. While we praised God for the expanded opportunities provided through the vision and support of our senior pastor, Gordon Kirk, we began to do less hands-on praying during class time itself.

So when a new class member, Paul Kupferman, requested prayer for pain in his left hip and lower back on February 23, 2002, it seemed like it had been quite some time since a similar situation had presented itself. Paul's job as a security guard kept him standing and walking about eight miles daily, he explained, aggravating the discomfort.

Dave and Brenda, wife of class vice-president Ralph Beas, knew how Peter Wagner would pray. Back and skeletal pain is sometimes tied to an apparent difference in leg length. Although Peter acknowledges that only medical professionals can measure limbs accurately, he almost invariably begins ministry with an informal check. He asks people requesting prayer to sit squarely in a hardback chair and allow him to lift their feet straight out in front. By putting their heels together he gets an idea of whether their legs are the same length. If not, he prays a prayer of command in Jesus' name for the short leg to grow to match the other. Then he goes on to intercede for relief of pain.

When Dave and Brenda heard Paul Kupferman's request, their faith soared to pray for the fifty-six-year-old Messianic Jewish believer. They asked him to sit while Dave knelt in front, cupped his hands behind Paul's heels, and lifted them forward.

"Did you know your left leg is about half an inch shorter than the right?" he asked Paul.

"No," Paul replied, sounding surprised. Yet the soles of his shoes clearly did not line up.

Turning his toes to each side, Paul watched the move of God for himself. With Brenda agreeing in prayer, Dave asked the Lord to release his power, then commanded the short leg to grow out. Before their eyes it did, pretty fast.

Everyone rejoiced. "The Lord's power is present for healing," Dave declared, in echo of Luke 5:17. "Let's pray for your hip and back now." Paul stood while Dave and Brenda laid their hands on him, asking God to heal. Nothing dramatic happened immediately, so the two just prayed for the Lord's continued blessing on Paul, trusting that his work in bringing symmetry to Paul's legs would help his aching body.

The next week Paul returned and said his pain had completely dissipated. He even ran on the beach and felt fine. Months later he remained pain-free.

Did God create new bone and tissue in Paul's leg? People who pray for limbs to grow realize that in most cases the Holy Spirit's work involves an adjustment or realignment of the skeleton. Either way, the healing brought glory to God as a tangible sign of his supernatural power, and rekindled my desire to pray and believe in the Lord for signs and wonders of all sorts.

Finding Out What God Is Doing

Even though I grew up in a large, evangelical church, hands-on prayer for healing did not become part of my experience until college. Bible stories and testimonies from missionaries who spoke in Sunday school left the impression that most miracles happened only long ago or far away.

Things began to change in high school, when a few people from my congregation, Glendale Presbyterian Church in Glendale, California, visited healing services held by evangelist Kathryn Kuhlman at the Shrine Auditorium in Los Angeles in the early 1970s. Some of their reports were astonishing. One of my friends and her father brought another teenage girl to a meeting, and the girl's buck teeth straightened out on the spot.

My later journey through charismatic prayer meetings opened my worldview to the possibility that contemporary signs and wonders could occur more frequently and closer to home than I imagined. Then when Dave and I met Peter Wagner at the 120 Fellowship class in 1984, he taught us how to embrace faith for an active ministry of the Holy Spirit without abandoning Bible-centered evangelical theology.

The more I learned, the more I saw that God's work in signs and wonders has continued throughout history, to the present day, and that he often uses ordinary people as his agents in conveying the blessing of such ministry to others. The Lord's promise in Joel, cited by Peter at Pentecost in Acts 2:17-21, reveals his intention to pour out his Spirit on all people, from lowest to greatest. Jesus chose as his apostles common folk— fishermen and businessmen—rather than rabbis or spiritual leaders. By not restricting ministry to certain ranks or positions, God has enabled the work of his Spirit to flow more widely to many more people, especially those not yet saved.

My interest in missions attracted me to numerous modern-day accounts of God using power ministries to bring people to salvation through his Son. Especially in cultures whose world-view allows for interaction between natural and spiritual realms, report after report tells of individuals, families, and whole communities giving allegiance to Jesus after some supernatural event pointed them to him. My book *Stories From the Front Lines: Power Evangelism in Today's World,* documents forty recent stories from around the world about the Word of God through the gospel teaming with the works of God through signs and wonders to lead people to faith in Christ.

The book in your hands developed in conversation with senior editor Kathryn Deering at Servant Publications, with the goal of training a spotlight on the signs and wonders God is performing for his glory even in our contemporary Western society. North American Christians who come to believe supernatural events take place today, not just long ago, may still think most miracles occur far away, in simple cultures unlike our own. The truth is that the current move of the Holy Spirit in power covers all corners of the globe. The United States has witnessed tremendous works of wonder, and will see many more as the return of Jesus Christ draws closer.

These stories—previously unpublished or in limited circulation—come from all over the country, from Los Angeles to Philadelphia, from Georgia to Oregon. There are accounts from men and women, from children, young people, and seniors. The people involved include Latinos, African-Americans, and Asians. Some of the events described took place in pentecostal, charismatic, or independent churches, others in mainline denominational settings. A few stories involve visible leaders with international ministries; most feature "just folks" like you or me.

In many cases primary sources with medical records can document what happened, before and after. Other cases turn on the reliability of credible witnesses. No matter where a sign or wonder took place, careful research and reporting of the evidence magnifiy God's glory by establishing verifiable facts as a safeguard against the story turning into mere legend when details fade or are changed in retelling.

What Are Signs, Wonders, and Miracles?

A "sign," defined in Greek as a mark or token, distinguishes and authenticates divine activity and points people to God. A "wonder" causes a beholder to marvel in astonishment or admiration. The term "miracle," whose English root suggests something to be gazed at in wonder, in the New Testament is most often translated from the Greek *dunamis,* referring to power or mighty works.

The three words often function interchangeably. Many people use the phrase "signs and wonders" as an umbrella term for all kinds of supernatural displays of power, and consider miracles a large subset of such events, usually objectively observable. Other signs and wonders that might not be classified as miracles could include more subjective supernatural experiences, such as dreams, visions, trances, visitations, angel encounters, and prophetic words of knowledge. Some consider progressive healing as a sign or wonder while specifying instantaneous healing as a miracle.

While God may act in supernatural power for any reason that promotes the purposes of his will, he often performs miracles and signs for the benefit of both believers and nonbelievers. They come frequently as blessings that meet some felt need—

for health, strength, guidance, reassurance, protection, or the like. As such, they demonstrate God's love and concern for the ones involved, and exalt him and his character.

Signs given to nonbelievers usually have the additional purpose of pointing them toward the truth about God and the gospel of Christ. Jesus invited people to consider his miracles in the process of discerning his identity: "Believe me when I say that I am in the Father and the Father is in me; or at least believe on the evidence of the miracles themselves" (Jn 14:11). The apostle Peter made the same point in his Pentecost sermon: "Jesus of Nazareth was a man accredited by God to you by miracles, wonders, and signs, which God did among you through him" (Acts 2:22). Paul and Barnabas had a similar experience on their missionary journeys, "speaking boldly for the Lord, who confirmed the message of his grace by enabling them to do miraculous signs and wonders" (Acts 14:3).

Not all supernatural events come from God, however. Second Thessalonians 2:9 states that Satan also operates "in all kinds of counterfeit miracles, signs, and wonders." To help us distinguish the godly from the ungodly, we do well to ask, "Does this sign or wonder glorify God and exalt Jesus Christ?" Miracles of divine origin will bear witness to the Lord and his character.

Heavenly miracles also produce some kind of good fruit that brings God glory. In Luke 6:43-44 Jesus describes this principle: "No good tree bears bad fruit, nor does a bad tree bear good fruit. Each tree is recognized by its own fruit. People do not pick figs from thornbushes, or grapes from briers." If a sign or wonder comes from God, the source will become known in the fruit as people draw closer to Christ and his kingdom, express greater love and commitment to him, walk in deeper holiness, or become motivated to pursue his purposes in their lives and ministries. Good fruit may ripen in the people involved in a supernatural experience, in others who hear about it, or in both.

Prayer for discernment will still prove useful, as some fruit may appear good at first glance but reveal core rottenness on closer inspection or passage of time. An initially attractive sign or wonder may actually draw someone into demonic bondage or deception. The Holy Spirit can lead us to the truth, as Jesus promises in John 16:13. The best and most unambiguously divine fruit comes in the form of souls saved for all eternity. Some of the stories in this book show God bringing salvation through mighty displays of power. When the Spirit's miracle-working activity mushrooms and begins to sweep more and more seekers into Christ's kingdom, revival is at hand.

Ministering in Signs and Wonders

Supernatural signs from God are sovereign acts, done through his will and power alone. Yet our heavenly Father responds to prayer and need. Many Scripture passages show the Lord waiting for someone to petition him in faith before he releases his will upon a situation. Recall Jesus' interchange in Matthew 8:2-3 with the man suffering from leprosy:

"A man with leprosy came and knelt before him and said, 'Lord, if you are willing, you can make me clean.'

"Jesus reached out his hand and touched the man. 'I am willing,' he said. 'Be clean!' Immediately he was cured of his leprosy."

In this case, a simple, believing request triggered a supernatural response in accord with divine will.

As a good Father, God also wants to train his children to do what he does. He has given us authority as his sons and daughters to exercise his will in his name. This commission includes ministry in signs and wonders. God receives more glory as more of his people participate more often in dispersing his divine power into the earthly realm.

Yet we must never forget where the power resides. Jesus states in John 15:5, "Apart from me you can do nothing." He also declares in Matthew 19:26 that "with God all things are possible." The apostle Paul echoes, "I can do everything through him who gives me strength" (Phil 4:13).

Without God—nothing. With God—everything. The key to praying in faith for the exercise of divine power is knowing God's will and purpose in a given circumstance. Jesus himself operated on this principle during his earthly ministry: "I tell you the truth, the Son can do nothing by himself; he can do only what he sees his Father doing, because whatever the Father does the Son also does" (Jn 5:19).

If the Father has not chosen to act in power, praying for a miracle will prove fruitless. Yet God often desires and waits for our cooperation in what he is doing and wants to do. In those cases, if we fail to pray and minister according to his will, we short-circuit an opportunity for him to receive glory through a demonstration of his omnipotence. Learning to hear and recognize his voice will help us keep in step with him, neither ahead nor behind, in any situation.

In ministering to unbelievers, or recounting to them stories about divine miracles, the connection between the power and the power source should shine forth clearly. For God to be glorified, we must lift up his name through the gospel of Christ. The effective partnership of Word and works, illustrated in Paul's ministry, will reap the greatest harvest of souls for God's kingdom.

The Wider Purposes

More than a collection of entertaining stories, this book aims to accomplish several purposes:

- By providing documented accounts of contemporary events in American culture, the book may provoke thought or discussion among those who tend to doubt modern-day miracles, or expand the scope of view of those who are open but unaware of all that God is doing among us today.

- The stories seek to build faith and encouragement that God's Spirit is here and moving among us, not just in other nations and cultures. If your prayers for societal transformation have sometimes flagged, these accounts may implant mustard seeds of faith that the Lord still has purposes to fulfill in America, and his mighty works of power are helping to prepare the ground for unprecedented revival.

- If you have harbored skepticism about media reports of miracles from various national or international organizations, you may gain a different viewpoint after reading the many stories about God working signs and wonders among ordinary believers. Despite an occasional hyped account intended to build someone's ministry reputation, most of the Spirit's supernatural activity today is taking place among common people with no desire for fame and no motive to exaggerate.

  By the same token, such stories can nurture hope that Almighty God may want to touch your own life, or the lives of your friends and family, with a supernatural display of his love and provision. If so, seek his will first, then petition him with the persistence of the widow in Luke 18:1-8.

- You might sense the Lord prompting your response of personal involvement. He may ask you to consider new avenues for the move of his Spirit, to intercede boldly for others, to offer ministries of healing prayer or deliverance through your church, or to welcome people whom God has gifted in signs and wonders, even if their backgrounds or styles differ from yours.

- Above all, this book aims to increase the worship and glory due to God for his immeasurable greatness. Countless Scripture passages urge and command us to declare his glory, to proclaim his character, to make known his deeds, and to record them for future generations. The more people hear about God's mighty acts, the more praise redounds to his name.

Let your voice join in magnifying the Lord and King of the universe as you read this small sampling of his awesome wonders taking place all around us today. As Psalm 34:3 exhorts us, "Glorify the Lord with me; let us exalt his name together"!

TWO

Miracles, Manifestations, and Divine Coincidences

MIRACLES COME IN all sizes and packages. Those involving physical health may range from instantaneous healing of a headache or terminal cancer (chapter 3 highlights such healing miracles) to restoration or creation of damaged or missing body parts (with an example or two in chapter 5) to resuscitation from death or near death (the focus of chapter 7). Other miracles might involve material objects doing strange things—an iron ax head floating, water turning to wine, a few loaves and fishes multiplying to feed thousands. Many people would also see the miraculous hand of God in simple coincidences of timing or circumstance that defy probability.

This chapter features a grab bag of manifestations of supernatural power. Some may seem more unbelievable than others. Yet recognizing and acknowledging a miracle depends less on the credibility of the evidence, important as that is, than on a worldview that allows for miracles in the first place. Those who start from the position that supernatural events do not occur today will not see any, no matter how much documentation is presented.

Jesus tells the story of the rich man who dies and goes to hell while the beggar Lazarus dies and ascends into paradise at Abraham's side. The once wealthy man, now in torment, begs Abraham to send Lazarus back to earth to warn the rich man's brothers to repent and avoid his fate. Abraham responds, "If they do not listen to Moses and the Prophets, they will not be convinced even if someone rises from the dead" (Lk 16:31).

Those with eyes to see will acknowledge the presence and power of God in numerous situations. Others who allow that miracles are possible but rare will perhaps see them more often, once the Holy Spirit has widened their worldview past the limits of traditional Western intellectualism.

The Bible encourages us, before we accept whatever is presented, to make careful examination of facts, to search the Scriptures for corroborating evidence, and to exercise discernment. Those who do so in an honest quest for truth, even if initially skeptical, will often find the evidence for God's presence and power too compelling to dismiss.

May the Lord use these stories, documented from firsthand reports of credible witnesses, to help open seekers' eyes to his wonderful works in our midst today.

Miracle on the 134 Freeway

Wednesday, August 11, 1999, dawned gray and misty—unusual weather for a Los Angeles summer day, although the overcast would burn off before long. In Burbank, California, on the eastern edge of L.A.'s San Fernando Valley, Araceli Alvarez finished her morning Bible reading and prayer and prepared to leave for work. At about six o'clock she climbed behind the wheel of her 1986 Chevy Nova. The little blue four-door had served her well, racking up mileage as she commuted to her job in Pasadena, about fifteen miles east.

Light traffic at that hour allowed Araceli to cruise in the fast lane with the speedometer topping sixty-five. As she headed down Interstate 5 and transitioned onto the 134 Freeway, her mind still churned with the issues she had laid before the Lord that morning. For months she had wrestled with the option of taking early retirement after her sixty-first birthday the following October. Her position as human resources data analyst at Kaiser Permanente Medical Care offered a good retirement plan, but her benefits would shrink if she left before age sixty-five. Elderly family members and a grown daughter sometimes needed Araceli's financial help. Would she be able to get by?

Friends at church who saw her ministry gifts urged her to

trust God to meet her needs. Araceli's leadership roles at Comunidad de las Américas, the Spanish-speaking congregation at Lake Avenue Church in Pasadena, kept her busy enough. Yet lately the Lord's favor and anointing had greatly expanded Araceli's prayer ministry of inner healing and deliverance. Partnering with her friend Juanita Cobb, Araceli constantly fielded requests for prayer from people seeking freedom from spiritual bondage. The pair, trained under the deliverance ministry of Doris Wagner at Global Harvest Ministries, found the demand for help overwhelming, and at the moment, they could schedule prayer sessions only outside of Araceli's long hours at work.

Araceli's background made her especially effective at this kind of ministry. As a youth in Cuba she had been groomed to become a high priestess in Santería, an occult religion. After coming to the United States in 1961, she had continued practicing witchcraft until a dramatic encounter with Jesus Christ in the summer of 1984 delivered her from this bondage and deception. The Lord soon gave her tremendous spiritual authority to minister freedom to others. By early 1999 Araceli and Juanita had begun the process of incorporating their own nonprofit organization, Fountain of Freedom Ministries.

Araceli recognized how her job limited the time she could devote to ministry. Many people who called for prayer had to wait weeks for an appointment. Yet the thought of leaving the security of a regular paycheck gave her cold chills.

Still, she sensed the Lord nudging her to boost her faith. *Can you trust me, Araceli?* he seemed to whisper. For years Araceli's greatest concerns had surrounded her daughter, Beatriz. She remembered BeBe's accident about eight months earlier, when her little Honda had been crushed between an old Cadillac and a pickup truck. The Cadillac's gasoline tank had ruptured, spewing fuel over BeBe. Yet she had managed to crawl out through a window, and the gas never ignited. When her mom tearfully hugged her later that day, Araceli heard the Holy Spirit's assuring words, *See—when you cannot take care of her, I will.*

Now Araceli felt additional urgency to make a decision about full-time ministry. After she had attended a deliverance conference in Colorado Springs in late July, her sense had grown that God was claiming her time for his purposes. Yet she continued to bargain with him. "Lord," she pleaded, "if you will arrange the finances and insurance and prove to me that you'll be with me in every way and that you really want me in this ministry, I will go."

Bang! About halfway into her commute that overcast August morning, a loud, unfamiliar sound from her car interrupted Araceli's musings. *What in the world?* she wondered. *Did I just run over a huge stone?* She felt no change in the car's handling, but the sudden bang had so startled her that she decided to pull over and check to see if anything was wrong. From the left lane she slowed and eased to the right, taking more than a mile to transition across the four lanes. Just beyond the Glendale Boulevard overpass, she parked the Nova on the shoulder, a little past the on ramp.

Araceli got out carefully. As she shut her door, another sharp bang made her heart jump. This time the right rear end of her car dropped to the ground. With growing trepidation she walked around to the passenger's side. What she saw did not compute. Her car rested on the end of a broken axle. Just to the right, the wheel with the tire lay on its side, about two inches of axle sticking up like a child's top. In between sat a neat pile of nuts and bolts.

Araceli squeezed her eyes shut and then stared again. *What is this? How is it that my axle broke right here on the shoulder? What was that loud bang a mile back?* She could only conclude that from the moment of a major axle failure, an angel must have held her car together until it was safely parked.

Some moments passed before Araceli's emotions calmed enough for her to use the roadside emergency call box to contact the auto club. She tried to explain that she would need more than the usual tow truck.

"Do you need a flat tire changed?" the dispatcher asked.

"No, the axle is broken," Araceli replied.

"What! Did you have an accident? Did you hit anybody?"

"No."

"Are you in the middle of the freeway?"

"No."

"Oh, if you're on the shoulder then you must have a flat tire."

"No, sir, I do not. The axle is broken."

The dispatcher expressed his doubts and the conversation cycled a few more times before Araceli finally said, "Fine, whatever you think—just send a tow truck that can lift the car completely."

After about twenty minutes' wait in the chill morning air, a truck arrived. Araceli praised God to see it was a flatbed—but she soon learned that this was a "coincidence" of the Lord's making. The dispatcher had called for a simple tire change, but the flatbed happened to be the nearest truck available.

The driver, Bob, took Araceli's information. Then he said, "Why don't you wait in the cab while I change your tire?"

"Sir, it's not a matter of changing a tire."

Bob's eyebrows lowered skeptically. "Well, let me take a look at it."

Araceli climbed into the tow truck, too spent to argue. A few seconds later, Bob came knocking at the window.

"Ma'am, you have a broken axle!"

"Yes, I know."

"Did you just enter the freeway from Glendale Boulevard?"

"No, sir. I've been driving from Burbank, and I first heard a loud bang more than a mile back in the fast lane."

"But, but ..."

Araceli explained how she had slowed and parked, and how the wheel had fallen off only after she had shut her car door.

The truck driver listened with an expression of total bewilderment. "You know, lady," Bob told her, "I've been in this business twenty-five years, and I have never seen a broken axle on a moving vehicle that didn't cause an accident, where the wheel didn't fly off. If you were going even forty-five in the right-hand lane, you would have hit the fence, and the wheel would have ended up who knows where."

Araceli just kept nodding. "I know, I know."

"Lady, you are very lucky," Bob said.

"No," Araceli replied, "I am very blessed. I'm telling you, sir, this is a miracle. The Lord saved me from a big accident."

Still looking dazed, the tow driver hoisted the wheel and laid it in the Nova's trunk. He collected the nuts and bolts, too, remarking about how they were not scattered or missing. "This can't be," he muttered. Then he lowered the back end of the flatbed and placed a small dolly under the broken axle before attaching cables to the car to pull it aboard.

Even though the distance to Araceli's home just exceeded the mileage limit of her insurance coverage, Bob agreed to take her there with no extra charge. He seemed to want to talk more about what he had seen. Back in Burbank, he left the Nova in Araceli's driveway, resting the axle on the ground. The next day she called her mechanic, who sent another flatbed tow to bring it in to the shop.

As Araceli processed what had happened, she could not miss a clear message from the Lord. *I am with you, Araceli. I told you I could take care of you. If I'm asking you to quit work, if I'm asking for your whole time, I will be with you.*

Araceli's faith grew to new heights as she considered how God had supernaturally saved her life. She applied for early retirement. In early 2000 she and her friend Juanita completed the incorporation of Fountain of Freedom Ministries. Their prayer sessions multiplied. Araceli started receiving invitations to teach on inner healing and deliverance.

Finances remain tight, and each day situations challenge Araceli's faith and trust. Yet whenever she feels anxiety rising about the future, the worry evaporates as she recalls the morning God or his angels held together her broken axle.

Divine Confirmation in a Box

Bryan Kessler loved Angie Wicker. Never before had he felt so sure he wanted to marry someone. And the best part was, he knew Angie felt the same way about him.

Ever since they had met on a blind date in August 1998, Bryan had sensed something special about the relationship. At six feet, three inches, twenty-six-year-old Bryan towered over Angie, who stood just two inches over five feet tall. Blonde-haired Angie, three years younger, seemed to look up to him in more ways than one. Week by week they grew closer. By December, Bryan began plotting how he would pop the question.

An hour's drive separated Bryan's home in Marietta, Georgia, from Angie's in Grayson, east of Atlanta. Most Wednesday nights they met about halfway, at their favorite Starbucks coffeehouse near Gwinnett Place Mall. From there they went out to dinner, savoring the conversation as much as the food.

Bryan picked the date he wanted to ask Angie to marry him: December 16. He decided to lead up to the event by presenting her with a series of gifts. One of the first things he had in mind to get her was a pair of gold cross earrings.

On Wednesday, December 9, one week before the planned engagement date, Bryan arrived at his work site in Alpharetta, where he did computer consulting for Xerox Connect. He asked his manager, Tim Beard, if he knew of a Christian bookstore nearby that sold cross jewelry.

Tim scratched his head. "Not that I know of," he replied. "But my wife's favorite jewelry store is James Avery Craftsman. It's got a lot of quality Christian and religious designs." Tim gave Bryan directions to the store, only a few blocks away.

By the time Bryan's lunch break arrived, morning stresses had clouded his mood to match the gray, rainy skies outside. He decided to drive the short distance to the store, not feeling very spiritual about his errand. Yet as he walked through the shop door, he sent up a quick prayer, "Lord, please show me what to get."

Intending to examine James Avery's selection of gold cross earrings, Bryan began scanning the showcases. Only a few minutes passed before his eyes lit upon a small, gold cross pendant. The design featured two nails fixed at right angles, their shape reminiscent of the spikes that fastened Jesus to the cross of Calvary. The pendant captured his attention and would not let go. Even though he had come looking for earrings, Bryan knew immediately he had to get this pendant for Angie.

That evening after work, Bryan headed for their usual Starbucks. When Angie greeted him, he could not tell if she saw any special glint in his eye. Then as they got into his car to go to dinner, Bryan brought out the box from the jewelry store.

He was a little afraid she might get the wrong idea. "I want to give you this," he said as he presented Angie with the box, "but I can tell you, it's not an engagement ring."

She cast him an intrigued glance and began to open the gift. When she saw the cross pendant, she caught her breath and froze. "Oh, my gosh!" she finally stammered.

Angie turned to Bryan in the driver's seat, a stunned look on her face. "Did you talk to anyone about this?" she demanded.

"No, why?" Bryan replied.

"Did you talk to my mom?"

"No, Angie—I don't know what you're talking about."

Angie paused, as if to collect her thoughts, and then told Bryan a story. "Three years ago, I was at a James Avery Craftsman store—the one in Buckhead—with my mom. I saw this very same cross pendant there and was really attracted to the design, except it was in silver, and I preferred gold. Somehow a notion came over me, and I prayed silently right there in the store, 'God, let the man I marry buy this cross nail pendant for me—in gold.'" Angie took a deep breath. "I'd forgotten all about that day in the jewelry store until tonight."

The pair sat in shocked silence for several moments. Finally

Bryan managed to blurt, "Whoa—that's amazing!"

Overwhelmed with joy and wonder, he and Angie went out to eat at a restaurant in the mall. They didn't talk too much more that evening, however, each one's thoughts swirling to process what God had just done.

Later Bryan learned even more. When Angie got home that night, she showed her mother the pendant and reminded her of the experience in the jewelry store three years before.

"Angie," her mom said, "you never showed me the design you wanted. You told me about praying that the man you marry would give you this special piece, but you never told me which one it was."

"I didn't?" Angie replied. She suddenly realized that even if Bryan had talked with her mom, he could not have learned her secret. No one else in the world knew.

Bryan continued his plan of showering Angie with gifts, including a pearl ring the next Tuesday. By the time he presented her with an engagement ring on December 16, the event seemed almost anticlimactic. Both of them had known for a week exactly what God intended for their relationship.

Although Bryan had felt impressed that Angie was God's choice for him, he realized that with such an important decision it is not easy to banish all doubts completely. Yet the supernatural sign God gave through the gold cross pendant left no question in their minds he had brought them together to be husband and wife, confirming his will in an extraordinary way.

Bryan and Angie married on April 24, 1999, sensing the love of God and family surrounding them. The gold cross pendant became a touchstone of their new life together, speaking of God's promise to help them walk through any difficulties because of his presence and power in their marriage.

"Just as we can look back at the cross of Calvary and see what Jesus did for us," Bryan reflects, "so Angie and I can look back to this little gold cross and say, 'We know God has put us together, no matter what.'"

"God's Got Your Number"

Jolly Abraham hung up the phone with a smile. She enjoyed nothing better than sharing the love of Jesus with those who did not yet know him. As the Lord opened doors, she took every opportunity by phone, letter, or in person to befriend and reach out to others, especially fellow Indians.

Jolly and her husband, Tom Abraham, both came to the United States from Kerala state in southwest India. While each grew up with a Christian family background, not until October 1994 did the Lord fully capture Jolly's heart and bring her into an understanding of biblical truth. She grew into ardent faith and was baptized the next May, at age thirty-five.

From their home in Skokie, Illinois, Jolly began talking about Jesus to friends and acquaintances as he drew her attention to them. In particular, she remembered a young Hindu man she had often served at her previous job as a teller at CoAmerica Bank (now LaSalle National Bank) in Skokie. Biju Krishnan, a slim eighteen-year-old, also came from Kerala, so Jolly naturally struck up conversations with him when he stopped in to make financial transactions. She had not seen him since she had left the bank in August 1994 and gone to work for a temporary employment agency. Yet now, following her salvation and baptism, she made a point of looking up his telephone number to share the Good News. A couple of times they made contact by phone, and Jolly felt that he responded with openness.

In 1996 Jolly dreamed she saw Biju standing before a group of people preaching the gospel. She recorded the dream in a notebook, excited about what it might mean. It spurred her faith that the Lord had great plans for this young man. Yet as the years passed and Jolly became involved with others, the dream faded from her mind and she lost contact with Biju.

Jolly took a position with W. W. Grainger, an industrial tool distributing company in Niles, Illinois, as an accounts receivable specialist. Late on Wednesday morning, August 8, 2001, she phoned the accounts payable department for Alcoa, Inc., a customer in Newburgh, Indiana. The accounts payable contact number was in Pennsylvania, so she carefully punched the phone pad: 1-412-553-2360.

"Hello, Abrix," came a man's voice on the other end of the line.

Jolly hesitated. "Uh, I'm calling for accounts payable?"

"No, I'm sorry; you've got the wrong department. I just picked up my colleague's phone as he's away from his desk. What number did you want?"

"I was phoning accounts payable at Alcoa—Aluminum Company of America, 1-412-553-2360," Jolly replied.

The man fell silent a moment. "Jolly? Is that you?"

Suddenly a jolt of recognition struck Jolly. "Biju? Biju Krishnan? How incredible to hear your voice again! Where are you?"

"Jolly, I work at Abrix in Northbrook. The number you reached is 1-847-498-8920."

Northbrook! Jolly's mind reeled. *Less than ten miles north of here!* "But Biju," Jolly answered, "how can that be? I was calling out of state. Your number is nothing like what I dialed."

As they talked and expressed their mutual astonishment, Jolly could come to only one conclusion. "Biju, this is the work of the Lord, putting me in touch with you again."

"Yes, I believe so," he agreed.

She pressed on. "Biju, I know Jesus loves you and he is calling you to his purposes. He has his eye on you and will not forget you or let you go."

Biju responded slowly, "It seems somehow God has shown favor to me."

The two reconnected with a bit more conversation, and eventually returned to their duties. All afternoon Jolly marveled at the Lord's supernatural intervention. However, God was not finished yet.

That evening at home, Jolly's phone rang. It was Biju.

"Jolly, you won't believe what else happened today," he said.

"About an hour after your call I sent a fax to one of my customers. Only it never reached them. I got a call back from someone saying he had received my fax in error. Because of my name, he was interested to talk. It turns out this man is a priest who works with churches in India! In fact, he recently came back from Trivandrum." With this link to a city in Biju's home state of Kerala, the priest had requested contact information for Biju's family in India.

Two divine connections in one day! Jolly shook her head in amazement as Psalm 139:7 came to mind: "Where can I go from your Spirit? Where can I flee from your presence?"

Biju gave Jolly his new home phone number and told her that in November 1999 he had married another young Indian, Priya. The two lived near the Abrahams in Skokie. He mentioned that Priya was looking for a job, and Jolly offered to pray that she would find one.

Jolly hung up the phone with more incredible news to share with Tom. The following week they invited Biju and Priya to a barbecue at their home. At the get-together about two weeks later, Priya informed them that a company had contacted her for a job interview right after Biju's call to Jolly, and she had been hired. The young couple enjoyed the Abrahams' hospitality, and Jolly presented them with a Bible.

The Krishnans and the Abrahams stay in touch. One step at a time Jolly prays and believes that the love of the Lord will manifest itself to them, and Biju will one day come into his divine destiny. In the meantime God has boosted her faith as she prays for family members and others to find relationship with Jesus Christ. Jolly recognizes that he is truly the all-powerful, all-knowing, and everywhere-present Creator, who has no trouble taking control of modern telecommunications technology.

Chase and the Duck

Stacy Daly eyed the overcast sky and felt on her cheeks the nip of nearly freezing air. From time to time the heavy clouds wrung out a sprinkling of cold rain, like giant gray sponges squeezed by unseen hands. She smiled, knowing what her husband, Clark, would say: It's a perfect day for fishing.

Clark worked rotating shifts as a firefighter, and was off duty that Thursday afternoon in March 2001. He often spent leisure time in serious fishing, but today's plans called for a fun and easy family outing at Bass Lake, about a fifteen-minute drive from the Daly home in Oakhurst, California.

Three-year-old Chase loved to go fishing with his daddy. The blue-eyed blond always wanted to try everything his dad did. Stacy, a stay-at-home mom in her mid-thirties, tagged along mostly to enjoy the time with her husband and son.

She helped load their red and white Ford F-250 pickup truck, and the family set out for the lake, winding into the Sierra Nevada mountains south of Yosemite National Park. The small to mid-size lake, normally drained to about half volume in winter, still held plenty of water for boating and for fish and ducks. Clark drove in toward the shore and parked close to the water on the sand, next to two of his friends from the Forest Service who had also come to Bass Lake that afternoon.

The Dalys greeted Clyde and Dennis. Chase shadowed his dad as Clark began setting up fishing poles in the dirt just in front of the pickup. Clark kept the truck's diesel motor and heater running so the cab could serve as a toasty refuge for his family.

Stacy stayed in the pickup most of the time, enjoying the scenery. She watched as half a dozen of Bass Lake's resident mallards flew over and landed in the water nearby. The drakes and hens know that visitors to the lake often bring food handouts.

Clark and Chase walked along the shore and checked the lines, periodically climbing into the cab with Stacy to warm up. On one of their excursions Stacy saw Chase point to the flock of ducks that had come onto the beach. Right away she noticed what had caught the toddler's attention: A little hen lagged behind the others, wobbling awkwardly as she waddled.

Hooked into her right foot was a large silver fishing lure, trailing a ball of tangled line and debris.

Clark tried to approach the injured duck, but she would not let him touch her. Chase waved his arms vigorously, calling to his dad. Before long the two of them joined Stacy again in the pickup.

"Mommy," a breathless Chase began, "that ducky is hurt! It has a fishing lure in its foot! Did you see it?"

"Yes, Chase," Stacy answered.

"I want Daddy to catch it," Chase went on, "so he can take the hook out of its foot."

"I saw Daddy try to help the duck," Stacy said, "but there's no way to catch her, Chase. She'll just run or fly away."

"Like I told you, son," Clark added, "wild ducks are too scared of people to let us hold them. We could never get close enough."

The boy's eyes clouded with concern. "But the ducky's hurt! It was walking funny. We have to help!"

Clark and Stacy exchanged sad glances as Chase went on about the bird's plight. They knew the hen would not live long when she had such trouble getting adequate food.

Stacy then spoke again. "All we can do is ask Jesus to help," she told her son. "Why don't you pray for God to take care of this ducky?"

"OK," Chase replied. The three-year-old's parents had prayed with their boy since infancy, teaching him how to talk to Jesus about all kinds of situations. "Dear Jesus," he said, "please help that ducky that's hurt. Please help us to catch it so we can take the lure out of its foot. Amen."

As Chase and his dad went back to check their lines, Stacy shook her head at her son's prayer. She knew Chase had great faith. Yet she had been thinking of simply entrusting the duck to God's care, not asking his help to catch the bird.

Over the next half hour or so Clark and Chase rejoined Stacy in the pickup a couple more times, warming and drying out when sprinkling rain started to fall. Chase kept insisting they try to catch the injured bird. Mom and Dad explained again how they could not just walk over and pick her up. They encouraged their boy to keep praying for the duck, asking Jesus to help her.

On their last excursion down the shoreline, Clark and Chase walked by the fishing poles of their friends in the next truck. Clyde and Dennis were also using their truck's cab as a weather shelter. Clyde got out to check his lines, and the Dalys watched him start to reel one in. Just then, without warning, the hen with the fishing lure skipped over the shallows and flew right into the line. Flapping and quacking wildly, the duck entangled herself.

Only a few yards away, Clark and Chase raced to the water's edge, where Clark took the bird into his arms. Instantly she became calm while he unsnarled the line. Clyde pulled a tool out of his pocket and went to work removing the lure from her foot. Stacy, meanwhile, could hardly believe her eyes, and got out of the pickup with a camera to record the scene.

By the duck's placid behavior and murmured quacks as the men labored over her, it seemed she knew they were trying to help. When they got her loose, Clark handed the bird to Chase, who held and petted her a moment before she flew off.

Chase began jumping with joy. "The ducky's free!" he cried as he watched her swim nearby with newfound energy.

The adults stood together, blanketed with wonder. Clark told his buddy, "Chase was so concerned about that duck, he actually prayed God would help us catch her so we could take that lure out."

"Whoa, that's awesome," Clyde mumbled.

Stacy wondered if Clyde—and Dennis, who had seen every-thing from their truck's cab—really understood how the God of the universe cares about injured ducks and the concerns of three-year-olds. Yet she knew they would not soon forget what had happened.

The Dalys collected their gear and headed home, chatting

about the duck all the way.

"Isn't God great?" Stacy said to her son. "Let's thank him for answering your prayer, Chase!"

The toddler folded his hands. "Thank you, Jesus, for helping the ducky! Amen!"

Stacy sensed that she and Clark felt more amazed at this miracle than did their faith-filled son. To this day they marvel as they recall the afternoon at Bass Lake when God moved supernaturally to answer a little boy's prayer.

Wind, Rain, and the Touch of Angels

The 1993 Honda Civic DX motored up Interstate 5 through California's Central Valley, carrying Bryan and Mercedes Marleaux north from their home in Corona del Mar in Orange County. Almost 450 miles later, the little black car transitioned into the city of Oakland. The Honda still had gas in its tank, but Bryan and Mercedes felt like the two of them were running on fumes.

The exhausting, all-day drive wearied their bodies, especially as they entered Bay Area traffic congestion. Yet other issues weighed on their minds. As itinerant evangelists with Grace World Mission, the Marleauxes often deal with challenging financial situations. They preach the gospel and minister in the power of God wherever he tells them to go, in the United States or internationally, trusting him to provide. The invitation for this current trip, for instance, came without discussion of honorarium or other compensation.

Yet that November of 1998, thirty-five-year-old Bryan faced daunting student loan bills from his master's degree program at Fuller Seminary in Pasadena. With no guaranteed paycheck, he could not see where funds would come from. Once again, God was teaching him and Mercedes to walk by faith, not by sight.

The little storefront church in Oakland, called the Assembly of God, hosted an independent Spanish-speaking congregation not affiliated with the similarly named denomination. Mercedes, a native of Argentina and herself a gifted preacher, would minister side by side with Bryan, translating for him during this three-day campaign.

"Looks like we're going to be late," Bryan muttered as the clock ticked past the 7:00 P.M. scheduled start of the opening meeting that Friday night. By the time they found the church, nestled in a run-down neighborhood, it was almost half past seven. As they parked, a sign across the street on a mortuary building caught Bryan's eye: "Fuller Funerals," it read.

He stared at the words. *OK, Lord, are you trying to send me a message?* In the midst of his discouragement Bryan sensed the Holy Spirit wanting to take him—once again—through a death process, teaching him not to rely on his own easily depleted strength and resources. A verse from his message for that evening rose to mind: "My grace is sufficient for you, for my power is made perfect in weakness" (2 Cor 12:9).

The two peeled themselves off the car seats and went inside with a box of materials to set up on a table in the back of the room. They heaved sighs of relief that the worship team was still leading, and Mercedes went to let someone know they had arrived.

Pastor Ricardo Puell greeted them warmly. His congregation of about 150 had invited another pentecostal church in nearby Alameda to attend the weekend campaign, and many had brought guests, so perhaps 250 people nearly filled the room.

Bryan's message that night centered on God's all-sufficient grace. When the couple finished preaching, they asked the Lord to release his anointing for ministry. Despite their exhaustion, they moved into the congregation and began to pray for people. In the midst of their weakness, God showed up with divine grace and power.

Several people throughout the room began to tremble and fall under the manifest presence of God, even before Bryan and Mercedes touched them. Folding chairs were moved to the side. The pair saw many people resting on the floor, with the

Holy Spirit evidently ministering to them in deep ways. As they prayed for others, several collapsed hard and fast, as though struck by a bolt of electricity.

Bryan started to feel a gentle breeze blowing from the back of the room. Focused on praying for people, he didn't really pay attention to it. When the service finally wrapped up at about half past ten, however, several people approached him with similar accounts. "Did you notice that? I felt a breeze blowing through here...."

Then Bryan realized that the room had no windows, no open doors, no fans, and no air conditioning or heating ducts. He thought of the scene in Acts chapter 2, when the sound of wind from heaven filled the house where the apostles were staying on the Day of Pentecost. He and the others praised God for this sign of his presence.

The Marleauxes stayed that weekend in the home of a church family, Javier and Laura Rosas. The evangelists went to bed more convinced than ever that God can and wants to work through his children despite their weaknesses and lack of faith. After arriving in such weariness, they saw a move of the Spirit that far outweighed their expectations.

On Saturday night the manifestations continued. Bryan again preached on aspects of God's grace, emphasizing that we receive not only salvation but also spiritual gifts by grace alone. When he gave an altar call to trust Jesus as Savior, several people responded, including a guest of the Rosas family. Laura and Javier told Bryan later that they had been sharing the gospel with this friend for a long time, with no result. Encouraged by the demonstrations of God's power, they had felt prompted to invite him to the campaign meeting that night, where he accepted Christ.

During the ministry time the Spirit of God moved on many people in powerful ways. As the praise band played and Bryan and Mercedes went from person to person, they heard weeping, praying, and worship throughout the room.

Then Bryan felt a few light drops of liquid fall on his head and skin, as though someone had flicked water off wet fingers in his direction. He looked up from his prayers momentarily but again shrugged off the sensation without thinking much about it. Yet after the service several others shared that drops had hit them, too.

Laura Rosas, a slender Latina of no more than forty, felt the sprinkles and more. She told Bryan and Mercedes that after the drops fell on her she looked around, noticed no natural explanation, and continued worshiping. Then she described how a sudden overwhelming presence came over her, and she felt what she perceived as a large angel wing brush against her. The sensation of soft feathers seemed to charge her body with power, and she crumpled to the floor. There, she said, she had a strong impression that God was releasing upon her a number of spiritual gifts for ministry, including prophecy.

"Wow!" Bryan responded. "We've seen several manifestations of God's power in our ministry before, but I think this is the first time for raindrops and angel wings. Would you be willing to share that testimony at the meeting tomorrow morning?"

When she did, following the message, the Spirit of God again came upon her and many others. Laura began to weep and fell down. Mercedes knelt and prayed for her, while Bryan followed the leading of the Spirit as he moved on people in the congregation. Although Bryan's Spanish grammar skills remain rough, he now speaks the language well enough to pray for people in most situations.

Later Bryan was ministering with Mercedes near the front when a young woman of about twenty approached them to receive prayer. After a few moments she started to cry. Her sniffles became shaking sobs as the Holy Spirit evidently touched some deep places in her.

After the service, she told them more. Marysol Aleman lived in San Francisco but came across the Bay to attend the Assembly of God regularly. "While you were ministering to others, I was standing at my chair about halfway back," she said. "I felt some-body grip my hand and pull me out to the aisle and lead me toward the front. It felt just like someone had a hold of me, but I couldn't see anybody there, even though I kept looking around. I think it was an angel grabbing my hand to bring me forward to ask for prayer, because normally I wouldn't do something like that. I don't like being in front of people."

The Marleauxes made sure Pastor Puell heard Marysol's story. At the beginning of the last meeting, late Sunday after-noon, he told the congregation, "You know, we didn't have a special theme for this *campaña*, but God has given us one. It has been a *campaña* of signs and wonders."

An atmosphere of joy and celebration filled that final gather-ing. Javier and Laura Rosas' teenage daughter, Yesenia, had attended all the meetings but had seemed distracted earlier. Now, after hearing her mother's testimony that morning and seeing everything else God had done, she responded with great openness when her mom and the Marleauxes prayed for her. Her body began to shake, and the Spirit filled her in a fresh way.

During the last meeting, Pastor Bothi from the church in Alameda stood and invited the people to give a special offering to Bryan and Mercedes. "This couple ministers in Mexico, where there's not a lot of money to go around. So put away your 'dollar offering' and dig deep in your wallet so we can really bless them."

Thank you, Lord, Bryan prayed silently. Neither he nor his wife had said anything about their needs. Still, in such a ragged neighborhood, he didn't have high expectations for a large gift. Yet when the campaign ended and people began to clean the room and go home, the pastors presented the couple with a brown paper lunch bag full of cash and a few checks. The total represented a significant sum for both givers and recipients.

This miracle boggled their minds as much as any other. Without them making their situation known, God had answered their desperate cry for his provision.

Through sporadic contact with the church after the campaign, the Marleauxes learned that many attendees received new zeal for the Lord and his service. Marysol and others who experienced supernatural encounters were deeply blessed and encouraged by the manifestation of God's love to them. The Rosas family felt their walks with the Lord quicken with fresh vitality as God renewed their faith that he answers prayer.

Bryan remembers that weekend as an impressive demonstration of how God, in his grace, uses broken vessels to display the surpassing greatness of his own power and glory. The evangelist now understands better Paul's words in 2 Corinthians 12:9, "I will boast all the more gladly about my weaknesses, so that Christ's power may rest on me."

Supernatural Transplant: A Miracle of Love

As Theresa McCartney read the long e-mail, her heart filled with compassion. She realized her friend, Tami Leather, was writing simply to unload a serious prayer request. Yet Terry sensed the Holy Spirit stir something inside. *Lord, what are you asking me to do about this?*

Until December 2000, Tami and Terry had worked in the same department at Janssen Pharmaceutica in Titusville, New Jersey, about ten miles up the Delaware River from Trenton. That month the department had reorganized and moved to Springhouse, Pennsylvania, about twenty miles west. Terry had made the transfer, commuting from her home near the river in Yardley, Pennsylvania, but Tami had stayed in Titusville. The two used to talk and pray together, but now their contact came mostly via e-mail.

When Tami's long message appeared on Terry's computer screen at work in January 2001, she could sense her friend's anguish as she poured out her concern for Catherine Walsh, a woman who was like a second mother to her. Tami described in detail the dire situation of her "Aunt Cathy," dying of kidney disease. Cathy had been born with a nonfunctioning right kidney, but knew nothing of her impairment until infection in her left kidney had developed into septicemia in March 1998. This toxic blood condition had put Cathy in the hospital, clinging to the edge of life.

Cathy learned she would need peritoneal dialysis to survive until a kidney became available for transplant. The fifty-two-year-old wife and mother of a ten-year-old son saw her life take a slow, downward spiral. The recurring treatments of dialysis labored to clear her body of the poisonous fluids that collected in her peritoneum, the body cavity surrounding the organs in her trunk. Yet over time, multiple bouts of infectious peritonitis made the dialysis increasingly less effective. Without a kidney transplant, Cathy faced death through renal failure.

At the time of Tami's e-mail, Cathy, who lived in Medford, some twenty-five miles south of Trenton, was back in the hospital with another peritoneal infection. For almost three years she had been on the waiting list for a cadaver kidney and had never received a call. Her only sibling, her brother Charlie, could not donate because an auto accident many years before had left him brain-damaged, and Cathy now served as his guardian.

Tami wrote to Terry in her distress, explaining all this and asking her friend to pray. Soon after Terry read the message and felt the Spirit's gentle nudge on her heart, she composed a return e-mail.

"You mentioned that Cathy has type O positive blood," Terry wrote. "I'm O positive. I would be willing to give a kidney." She finished her note and pressed *Send*.

Minutes later Terry's phone rang. Tami was on the line.

"Terry, are you serious?" the young woman asked. "I have chills up and down my spine."

Terry assured her she was serious, and asked about the next steps. She also stressed that she did not want anyone to know about her offer. Terry remembered the instruction from Matthew 6:3-4, "When you give to the needy, do not let your left hand know what your right hand is doing, so that your giving may be in secret."

Tami obtained the phone number for the transplant coordinator at the University of Pennsylvania Medical Center. When Terry spoke with her, she found she would need to give blood samples for compatibility tests. Because Terry preferred to remain anonymous, she could not go to her usual care providers. Through Tami, Terry got the name of a nurse-midwife friend of Cathy, and phoned Viola late one Monday afternoon to see if she could come to the McCartney home to draw the blood.

Viola dropped by only ten or fifteen minutes later. Her visit caught Terry off guard, because she maintains a regular discipline of fasting and prayer on Mondays. Still, she went ahead with the sampling. The university had sent Terry a package with twelve vials in different sizes, totaling perhaps a third of a pint. As Viola drew blood from the petite fifty-two-year-old, Terry began to feel faint. After the twelfth vial, Terry slumped on the sofa, pale and weak.

Just then her husband, Bob, came home from work. Terry caught his look of consternation as he surveyed the scene. She had intended to tell him of her kidney offer only after she knew if her blood and tissue matched Cathy's. Now there was no way to couch the news. As soon as Viola left, Terry tried to explain. However, she saw her normally kind and gentle husband grow increasingly agitated.

"Terry! Your kidney? How could you give a kidney to a stranger? What if they take this one and something happens to the other? You'll be dead yourself!" Bob's voice rose and his face tensed with anger as he ticked off all the reasons Terry should reconsider her scheme. "The operation itself is a huge risk. And you're not a good candidate as an organ donor." Terry bit her tongue as he cited the evidence: too small, too frail, too old.

Terry knew her husband of thirty years loved her desperately, was concerned for her welfare, and felt helpless at the idea of standing by while she did something so radical and irreversible. Yet the Lord had planted in her an unshakable purpose. Over the coming weeks, as her husband and medical personnel kept asking why she was doing this, she replied, "I'm a follower of Jesus. God sent his Son to die for me. The least I can do is give a kidney as a gift of life to a dying woman."

Through the years Terry and Bob had both grown in their faith. Raised as Catholics, they now attended Washington Crossing United Methodist Church, where the gifts of the Spirit flowed in ministry. Walking the tortuous path of this kidney donation, however, would stretch each of them in new ways.

Terry learned that her blood had three of the six antigens in Cathy's blood, an excellent match from a nonrelative. As screening progressed, the medical staff gave her every opportunity to back out at any time. Bob continued to discourage her, and their two grown sons didn't like the idea any better. Yet Terry stood on the Scripture from Hebrews 12:2, "Let us fix our eyes on Jesus, the author and perfecter of our faith, who for the joy set before him endured the cross." She knew if she could keep her eyes on Jesus and the coming joy when her organ saved a life, she could endure.

Tami had told Cathy of an anonymous donor's willingness to give a kidney. Yet, as Tami relayed to Terry, Cathy never let her hopes climb too high. She knew the donor could change her mind up to the last moment. Besides, after wrestling with the "why me" questions for so long, she had come to put herself into God's hands, praying for the strength to accept his will, wherever the road might lead.

In April Terry went to the University of Pennsylvania for a full day of testing, including chest and abdomen X rays and more blood work. Twice she had had to collect her urine for twenty-four hours. Doctors took an MRI of her kidneys and did a renal scan to determine their functionality.

By this time Terry had decided to make contact with Cathy by phone. Cathy still did not know her donor's last name, but they began to learn something about each other and their backgrounds. They discovered much they shared in common. About the same age, both women were trained as nurses. Both had two sons, although Cathy had lost her older one, an Air Force pilot, in a helicopter accident more than ten years before. Like Terry, Cathy had been raised Catholic, and still attended that church with her husband, Jack.

In early May both women, with their husbands, went to the University Medical Center transplant office for pre-admission testing. In the waiting room Terry heard a familiar name called.

"Catherine Walsh."

Terry watched as the woman went in for her first test. When she returned to the waiting room, Terry could not resist approaching her.

"Catherine?" she said quietly. "I'm Terry McCartney. I'm your donor."

Cathy looked at her and began to weep. The two exchanged a long hug. They introduced their husbands also, although they had little time to talk that day.

As it turned out, several more weeks would pass before transplant surgery. That afternoon doctors called to say Cathy had had another bout of peritonitis. The operations would need to be postponed while antibiotics knocked down this latest infection.

Finally a new date was set: Thursday, June 28. As the day approached, Bob McCartney continued to question his wife's decision. At the same time, Terry's prayer partner—the only other person Terry had told, in order to receive the protective covering of her intercession—gave her some wise counsel. Rosamaría encouraged Terry, who desired Bob's blessing, to seek his forgiveness for not asking him and including him in the decision from the beginning.

The night before surgery, as they had supper together in their home, Terry did just this. Bob's attitude changed completely. He forgave his wife, prayed for her, and blessed her. When they left for the hospital the next morning, she felt his loving support.

At half past seven they said good-bye to each other and Terry was taken away. Yet for the next forty-five minutes she lay on her gurney in the hallway outside the operating room, and nobody came by. *Where is everyone?* she wondered. As she waited alone, she recalled the words of Jesus in Matthew 26:40: "Could you ... not keep watch with me for one hour?" His anguish became real to her.

Finally doctors and technicians arrived and ushered her into the operating room. They extended her left arm to insert an intravenous line, and strapped down her right arm with a blood pressure cuff. In that position, with arms stretched out on the operating table, Terry felt as though she were undergoing her own version of crucifixion. At her lowest moment, she too wondered, *Could not this cup pass from me?*

Her surgery lasted until three o'clock that afternoon. When Terry was transferred to her hospital room, her face and body had swollen with edema. The fluid buildup made her eyes feel like slits in a puffy face.

She rejoiced to hear that Cathy's surgery, started shortly after hers, had gone well. Terry's left kidney, implanted in her friend, began functioning almost immediately.

The next day, however, Cathy's husband, Jack, brought Terry heartbreaking news. Overnight nurses had noticed Cathy's urine production gradually diminish. When they took her for a renal scan, they found the kidney no longer working. The renal artery had kinked, shutting off the flow of blood to the kidney. With no blood supply, the tissue quickly began to die. Now Cathy faced a second surgery to remove the necrotic organ.

Devastated, Terry cried to the Lord, asking for a word of Scripture to pray for Cathy. In her distress she simply let her Bible fall open. There in Luke 14 she found the story of how Jesus healed a man with dropsy. Terry prayed healing for her friend. Not until months later did Terry look up exactly what dropsy meant. The definition she found was "an edematous condition; kidney disease..."

On Friday afternoon Cathy returned to the operating room. What happened next was a story Terry and Bob heard from the surgeon late that evening.

Cathy's surgeon, Dr. N., said that just before Cathy went under anesthesia the second time he expressed to her how sorry he was that the situation had not worked out. He had heard about the volunteer donor who had sacrificed her kidney in great faith, and now it was dead. Dr. N. and his team removed the blackened organ. He held the kidney, smaller than a fist, in his hand and prepared to discard it into a basin.

"Then," he told the McCartneys, "I looked down and saw love on that kidney."

Terry thought he was speaking figuratively—that he had contemplated her act of love in donating the organ. However, Dr. N. made it clear: He literally saw the word "love" on the kidney itself.

Something compelled the surgeon not to discard that kidney. In that instant, he told the McCartneys, he made a decision to do something he had never done in more than twenty years of practice. He announced to the rest of the surgical team that he was going to try reattaching the organ. Some objected that Cathy had already been under anesthesia for many hours, and what was the point of prolonging surgery when the organ had died? Yet Dr. N. wanted to try, and one surgical assistant supported his idea. The team went back to work.

When they got the kidney reattached and removed the last hemostat clamping off the blood, the organ pinked up almost immediately and urine began to flow. Everyone stood amazed at the sight. After a moment of complete silence, one member of the surgical team ventured to say, "I believe we have just witnessed a miracle."

Terry and Bob could hardly believe their ears at Dr. N.'s tale. Yet they later learned that after Cathy recovered sufficiently, he told her the same story. In fact, Cathy recalled, he added an awesome comment: Dr. N. said that he was a Muslim, but after what he had witnessed, he recognized the power of their God, Jesus Christ. He had felt the power and presence of God in that operating room.

On Saturday morning, Terry walked down the hall to visit her friend. Cathy lay asleep, but Terry smiled to see her urine bag filling. When they talked later, Cathy expressed her admiration for Terry's strong faith throughout the ordeal, and said, "I want to pursue knowing Jesus the way you do."

Terry went home late that afternoon, still very sore and swollen. Soon, however, she lost the excess fluid, and she regained her strength within a few weeks.

Cathy remained in the hospital for ten days as doctors watched for signs of organ rejection. A tiny leak from her bladder presented a temporary complication, but the hole sealed itself before long. Cathy has returned regularly for checkups, and lab work has consistently shown everything to be normal. She says she feels the energy of a woman ten years younger.

After the miracle God performed in the operating room, Terry felt released to share the story, for his glory. She and Cathy now testify at different churches, describing what the Lord did in each of their lives through this supernatural manifestation.

Cathy recounts how she used to think miracles happened only to people who deserved them. Instead of asking "Why me?" regarding the traumas of her illness, she now ponders "Why me?" as she considers God's purpose in sparing her life in such an amazing way. She shares honestly about his forgiveness of past sins, and how she has pressed in to increase her knowledge of the Lord and his Word.

As they testify Terry tells how she had prayed in the year before the surgery for God to enlarge her understanding of all Jesus did in dying on the cross for her, so she would never take that sacrifice for granted. Through her experience of sacrificing a kidney, she feels the Lord answered her prayer with unforgettable impressions. Just as Jesus faced opposition on his journey to the cross, Terry endured her husband's relentless attacks as he questioned her decision. They then shared a last supper together before she entered the hospital, when they reaffirmed their love and commitment. Terry underwent her own Gethsemane on the morning of the operation while seemingly abandoned in the hallway for the better part of an hour. She imagined herself stretched out on the cross during preparation for surgery. And then she saw resurrection when God restored what was dead.

Bob's heart, too, has changed. He now understands more fully how God the Father must have felt to watch his Son endure crucifixion and death.

Through the testimonies Terry and Cathy share, God has borne much fruit. Many listeners have declared that they will never be the same. Others have come to accept the Lord and his love for the first time.

In Isaiah 49:16 God says, "I have engraved you on the palms of my hands." Terry McCartney says, "God is love, and I believe he engraves his name on our organs, our hearts, our kidneys. He loves us so much that he gave his only Son to die for us. And to some small extent he has let me understand that in a miraculous way."

THREE

Healing Miracles

HEALING AND DELIVERANCE are "the children's bread," Jesus declared to the Canaanite woman in Matthew 15:22-28. By referring to such an everyday necessity in his metaphor, Jesus seems to indicate that such wonders should be part of the staple diet of believers, not occasional treats granted when Dad feels especially benevolent.

Earlier, in Matthew 7:9-11, Jesus described the Father's eager readiness to give such bread and other blessings to his children: "Which of you, if his son asks for bread, will give him a stone? Or if he asks for a fish, will give him a snake? If you, then, though you are evil, know how to give good gifts to your children, how much more will your Father in heaven give good gifts to those who ask him!"

Jesus' own earthly ministry highlighted healing as a common expression of the love and compassion of God. By meeting the physical needs of hurting people, he showed concern not just for their souls' salvation but also for their immediate pain and suffering. In the process, he demonstrated the power of God and drew people to faith.

While all divine signs and wonders bring glory to the Lord for his sovereignty and omnipotence, perhaps none more than healing glorify him also for his heart of mercy. Despite the brevity of our earthly lives in light of eternity, the God of the universe cares about relieving our temporal distress. No wonder so many people in the Bible who experienced his healing ministry gave their lives to follow him.

Since 1 Corinthians 12:9-10 distinguishes between gifts of healing and miracles, some have suggested divine healing normally takes place as a process, whether short or long, while instantaneous healings can be classified as miracles. All kinds of healing deserve our gratitude to a loving and mighty God—but some make more dramatic stories than others. The following accounts feature people who received the Great Physician's touch in a sudden moment of supernatural power.

"The Films Must Be Wrong": Confounding the Doctors

Two pounds, ten and a half ounces.

Matthew and Amy Maiberger, overwhelmed with the joy and anxiety of first-time parents, could hardly comprehend it. Their son, Gabriel, born ten weeks early, weighed less than a pitcher of orange juice.

His live birth on August 23, 1998, represented a miracle in itself. Unbeknownst to twenty-three-year-old Amy, she had been carrying twins, one of whom died eight weeks into term. Then a rupture in her amniotic sac caused its precious fluid to leak out. At her twenty-week ultrasound, her obstetrician found the sac empty of fluid, yet still detected Gabriel's heartbeat. She rushed to send Amy to the high-risk clinic at the University of Michigan Medical Center at Ann Arbor, near the Maiberger home in South Lyon. She could not get an opening until the next day, and with no amniotic fluid, doctors expected the second baby, too, would soon die.

That night, however, pastors and elders from their church, where Matt serves as youth pastor, came to pray for them. Brighton Christian Church, some fifteen miles north of Ann Arbor, was a rapidly growing congregation of about 350 at the time. When the high-risk pregnancy clinic performed the ultrasound, they found fluid in Amy's amniotic sac—about one-third full.

Doctors discovered that the rupture was high on the sac, so it repeatedly filled with fluid, then leaked. They could do nothing but wait and hope Gabe continued to grow. When Amy went into labor at thirty weeks, they let the baby come—ready or not.

The Neonatal Intensive Care Unit (NICU) became a second

home for the couple as they visited Gabriel daily. Family and friends from church received authorization to come and pray as often as they wanted. The tiny baby spent seven weeks on a ventilator, then endured a few more weeks on a device called CPAP, which provides Continuous Positive Airway Pressure.

By mid-November, when the CPAP was replaced by an ordinary oxygen cannula in Gabe's nose, Matt and Amy felt confident their baby was out of danger and would come home before long. Matt specifically prayed for his homecoming as a Christmas present.

Then in late November they noticed his blood oxygen saturation levels taking ominous dips. While healthy adults usually have oxygen saturation levels of 98 to 100 percent, NICU babies do well to maintain levels anywhere in the 90s. In a few days Gabe's saturation declined from about 94 to 92 or 91, then dropped to 89 or 88, then hit the mid-80s—despite the pure oxygen his cannula delivered. (Room air, by contrast, contains only 21 percent oxygen.)

Gabe's breathing became labored and irregular. The NICU team added an oxygen hood to help him. At the same time, he began coughing and gagging, occasionally vomiting the nutrients from his feeding tube. After their baby's steady progress for more than three months, Matt and Amy wanted to believe these developments represented only temporary setbacks.

On November 30 doctors performed a bronchoscopy, putting a tube with a miniature camera down Gabe's throat to examine his airway. As they studied the monitor on the scope and the films it produced, they determined that he had laryngomalacia, a condition sometimes called "floppy epiglottis." The epiglottis, normally a firm flap of flesh in the throat, acts like a trap door to seal the top of the windpipe during swallowing and open it during breathing. A collapsed or floppy epiglottis, however, can get sucked into the windpipe during inhalation, blocking air from reaching the lungs.

Gabe's doctors gave some hope that the epiglottis might firm up on its own over the course of a couple months or so. A few days later they removed the oxygen hood as they saw some progress. Yet the periodic gagging and vomiting persisted, and when Gabe's oxygen saturation levels dipped again in the second week of December, he went back under the hood.

On Monday, December 14, his team of physicians decided to consult the ear-nose-throat specialists. Afterward, Amy got a call from one of the ENT doctors: "I'm sorry, but Gabriel is going to need surgery tomorrow morning."

Amy, home alone that afternoon, nearly fell apart when she heard this news. After coming to believe that her son was on the homeward stretch, she felt as though time had turned back to the agonizing, touch-and-go days immediately following Gabe's birth.

The ENT doctor explained that the surgical team, depending on what they found, would choose one of two options. They might use a laser to cut away part of Gabe's epiglottis, in hope that this would solve the breathing interference. Yet the laser procedure carried the risk that a smaller epiglottis might not seal Gabe's windpipe sufficiently during swallowing; then aspiration of food and liquid into the lungs could cause infection. Alternatively, they might give Gabe a tracheostomy to deliver air to his lungs through a tube in his neck, bypassing the upper throat. Since Gabe's labored breathing increased his heart rate, the longer this trouble continued, the more he risked irreversible heart damage. A tracheostomy would provide a steady air supply and buy time for the epiglottis to mature and firm as Gabe grew. Yet such an invasive operation carried its own risks of infection and complications.

Either choice sounded horrible to Amy. Devastated, she phoned both Matt and the church office, her voice edged with panic as she spilled the news. She asked any available pastors and elders to come to the hospital that evening to intercede for Gabe. One of the pastors prayed with her, comforted her, and helped calm her fears. By the time she hung up the phone, Amy felt a sudden surge of peace and reassurance that God was both able and willing to heal Gabe. Her faith began to rise that the Lord wanted to do something that would bring him alone all the glory.

After dinner that evening, Pastor Tom Elliott and an elder, Jim Westerfield, met Amy and Matt at the NICU. Amy waited outside with Tom's little daughter while the three men went in to pray for Gabriel in his Isolette.

When Tom and Jim came out and retrieved Tom's daughter, they seemed upbeat and certain that the Lord had heard their prayers. Not until Amy joined Matt in the NICU herself, however, did she hear the whole story.

Even before she got to the bedside, she saw the change on Gabe's respiration monitor. Her son's labored breathing had previously traced a crazy, jagged line across the screen. Yet now the line had settled into steady, even bumps. Previously restless and struggling, Gabe now lay at peace.

Matt gave Amy the details about their prayer time. "And not only did Gabe's breathing return to normal, his oxygen sats started climbing. Take a look." Amy's excitement and anticipation swelled when she saw the figures on the equipment. By the time the two went home that night, they felt confident God was up to something big.

The next morning they visited their son before doctors gave him anesthesia and prepped him for his midday operation. The surgical team described their plan: "We're going to do another bronchoscopy to get a good look at Gabriel's current situation. Then if we decide on the laser option, we'll go right ahead, and inform you afterward. If we need to do a tracheostomy, we'll come let you know first."

Amy, praying specifically that the doctors would find nothing wrong and cancel surgery, sat on pins and needles as she waited expectantly for God to answer her prayer. Still, her heart jumped when the doctors entered the waiting room after only half an hour, holding films from the bronchoscope.

One of them, looking sheepish, said, "Mr. and Mrs. Maiberger, we don't know who did the previous films, but Gabriel's epiglottis is fine. We didn't perform either procedure, and he's coming out of the operating room now."

Amy could hardly restrain herself from leaping and hollering "Hallelujah!" The surgical team pointed out how the floppy epiglottis seen in the first set of films now looked firm and normal.

Matt, playing devil's advocate, asked, "How is this possible? Could Gabe's epiglottis have healed itself between the bronchoscopy two weeks ago and the one this morning?"

The surgeons scoffed. "If this condition were to correct on its own," one said, "there's no way it would heal in less than two months—let alone two weeks." They suggested that the previous films and tests had been flawed.

Matt and Amy shared a different conclusion. "Last night we and our pastors prayed," said Amy, beaming, "and we know Gabe was healed by God."

The doctors mumbled something like, "Well, we're glad you have faith"—clearly at a loss as to how to respond.

The couple returned to the NICU while awaiting Gabe's arrival from the operating room. There his primary care nurse on the day shift, normally warm and bubbly, looked pale and shaken.

"I heard they're bringing Gabe back—that they didn't do surgery," she blurted. "What's going on?"

Matt and Amy explained how they had prayed and God had healed.

"What? You're kidding! I mean, they didn't do anything?" the nurse stammered, eyes wide. "It's not possible! I was here when they did the first bronchoscopy. I saw the monitor. I saw the film. I watched his epiglottis being sucked in on the scope. It was in bad shape! How could this happen?"

Amy replied, "I'm sure you saw all that. The films were not wrong. But the Lord answered our prayers and healed him." She and Matt knew the nurse had seen folks from their church come many times to pray for Gabriel.

The redhead burst into tears as she heard about the manifestation of God's power. She asked Matt and Amy, "If God can do that for Gabe, do you think he can heal my mom?"

Matt and Amy learned a bit about the nurse's family needs and encouraged her to pray for her mother. She was not sure she had a Bible at home, so the Maibergers made plans to bring her a study Bible in a modern translation, embossed with her name.

After the cancelled surgery, Gabriel made such rapid progress that God answered another prayer: His parents brought him home on Christmas Day. They have faced some hurdles along the road to Gabe's good health, including a struggle to get him to eat enough, leaving him a bit skinny. And they trust that the growth of new, healthy lung tissue will increasingly compensate for tissue scarred by the ventilator during his first seven weeks of life. Yet, overall, Gabe is progressing well as a happy preschooler who loves to worship God.

Amy and Matt still recall a poster they used to see at the medical center, apparently part of a conference or campaign going on, that read in bold letters "KNOWLEDGE HEALS." They always laughed and declared the truth instead, a declaration that still echoes from their testimony: "No way! The Lord alone heals! He might use us in the process, but God is our healer, and to him alone be the glory!"

Planting Fruit for the Kingdom Through Healing Power

Renée LaZarrus headed to work on Saturday, October 10, 1998, unaware that her life would change that afternoon. At a nursing home across town in Rochester, Indiana, the petite twenty-one-year-old with dark hair and glasses worked as a nurse's aide in a ward of residents suffering from Alzheimer's disease.

Renée enjoyed her job. In fact, she enjoyed her life. She and her husband, Jeffrey, sixteen years her senior, had a delightful baby daughter, Kaylynn. They attended Faith Outreach Center, a Foursquare church in Rochester, and took part in various outreach activities, including prison ministry, street preaching, and itinerant evangelism. Jeff's factory work paid the bills, but they both knew he had a calling to minister full time. Renée, also gifted in evangelism, served right alongside him.

She arrived at the nursing home for her 2:00 P.M. shift and began her usual routine of checking residents, making sure everyone took a turn in the bathroom, and getting them ready for the evening meal.

One resident had soiled his pants, not unusual for Alzheimer's patients. Renée helped John into the bathroom, set him down on the toilet, and explained that she was going to change his clothes. As she bent over to remove his pants, without warning he punched her squarely in the back. The blow, landing near the top of Renée's spine, knocked her to the floor and left her immobile. She felt something pop and an immediate rush of excruciating pain.

Renée cried out for help, but the bathroom door, which swung outward, was pulled nearly closed, and no one heard her. Above the injured young woman John now stood poised with clenched fist, ready to strike again.

She realized her only option was to talk him out of it. "John, you hurt me!" she scolded him. "Don't be a bad boy! I can't believe you did that, when you're usually a good boy. Why would you act like that?" Something inspired Renée to begin singing an old hymn, "Jesus Loves Me."

In a moment John sat down on the toilet and started to weep. Although her back muscles felt like gelatin, Renée knew she had to take this opportunity to get out. Somehow she crawled to the door, pushed it open, and rose to her knees before a nurse spied her and came to her assistance.

Renée never recovered. When she saw her doctor, he diagnosed severe damage to her muscles, tendons, and ligaments. The blow had pushed her spine out of alignment. Spasms in her horribly swollen back, neck, and shoulders caused aching knots. The doctor took X rays and prescribed pain medication, but could offer few recommendations other than bed rest and regular monitoring.

Moreover, the doctor surprised Renée after she told him how the injury had happened. John, it turned out, was also a patient of his. "Did you know in his younger years he was an accomplished martial arts instructor?" The doctor speculated that John's punch, had it come at a different angle, could have caused even more harm.

Renée now lived in constant agony, with limited mobility in her upper body. Jeff took over her duties at home and cared for his wife with wonderful patience, but their lives changed. Renée could no longer lift their baby girl to hold her; Jeff had to place Kaylynn into her mother's lap. Beyond this heartache, Renée grieved most that her injury kept her from raising her hands in worship to God.

A series of medical specialists suggested different treatments: physical therapy, massage therapy, cortisone shots, various narcotics, a TENS unit (used to mask pain), insertion of needles into her head and back. Nothing brought more than limited, temporary relief. Furthermore, the doctors told her frankly that none of these treatments would cure the problem.

One doctor eventually suggested a radical operation to inject a compound into her spine to replace Renée's ligaments and tendons artificially. Yet even this procedure would merely lessen the pain somewhat. Renée and Jeff declined, and concentrated on seeking the Lord for divine healing while learning to deal with Renée's disability in the meantime.

Friends at church and in the community continued to pray for them. Renée found that if she fought off hopelessness and maintained an attitude of trust in God to strengthen her, she could function better. In public she worked hard to keep her misery out of her countenance, so people who did not know her might not perceive the pain that lay beneath her stooped posture.

Because of complications caused by her powerful narcotics, Renée miscarried a baby in 1999. The next year, when she learned she was pregnant again, she had to stop taking all drugs and try to get by on massage therapy, hot baths, and prescription-strength lotion. Morphine helped her survive labor, and she delivered another beautiful girl, Rebekah Grace, on January 20, 2001.

Three months later their pastor at Faith Outreach Center, Dan Mundt, told Jeff and Renée he sensed a strong leading from the Lord that they should attend a Church Planter's Intensive training conference. "The church will pay for it," Pastor Dan said. "We really want you to go."

The four-day "boot camp" training in Illinois, led by Pastor Glenn Bleakney, confirmed God's calling on Jeff and Renée to full-time ministry. Jeff stepped out on faith and resigned from his job. The two prayed for God's direction as they pursued advice from Pastor Glenn and other church planters, although Renée had not felt open to tell them about her disability.

In August 2001, Pastor Glenn invited the LaZarruses to visit his church in Aurora, Illinois, to observe a church plant in progress. Solid Rock Church had already acquired a building, now under renovation for the group of core members Glenn was gathering.

Jeff and Renée and their two girls joined the twenty-five or thirty people at Solid Rock for their service on Sunday morning, August 26. A worship team led in praise, followed by Pastor Glenn's sermon. After his message, Glenn invited anyone wanting prayer to come forward.

Several people went up. Jeff made his way to the altar to seek God's direction in ministry, while Renée stayed in the pew with Kaylynn and Graci. Yet as Pastor Glenn and his wife, Lynn, began to pray for people, Renée felt a strong urge to go to the front with her husband. After making sure another woman nearby could keep an eye on the girls, Renée stood and started down the center aisle.

Just then Glenn finished praying for the man next to Jeff. He turned to Jeff, saw Renée coming forward, and pointed to her. "The Lord is going to heal your back," he declared. "The Lord is going to heal you this day." As if to confirm the supernaturally discerned word of knowledge, he repeated to Jeff, "The Lord is going to heal her back today."

Renée began to weep. When she reached the front, Jeff held her and they wept together as Pastor Glenn laid his hands on them and prayed against the affliction in Jesus' name.

Renée knew this was the divine moment they had waited for, although at first she felt no change in her intense pain. Still, she began to praise God for his healing power.

After a few minutes she needed to return to the pew where the woman had been sitting with Kaylynn and Graci. There Renée stood and continued weeping, praising God, and thanking him for what he was about to do. Soon a warmth poured over her, and her body began to move. She felt her spine rearranging and coming into alignment. Her shoulders shifted back from their rounded slump, and her back muscles strengthened to receive the shoulders. In a moment she realized her pain had completely disappeared.

The others in the congregation had fixed their eyes on Renée as soon as Pastor Glenn had spoken the word of healing. They cried and rejoiced with her when they observed the changes in her body. While the worship team resumed the music, Jeff returned to the pew. He took his wife into his arms and asked, "Is it done?"

"It's done!" Renée confirmed. "We're healed!" Again they wept together.

Renée heard God tell her clearly, *Now praise me!* She joined in singing, and raised her hands in worship for the first time in nearly three years.

By the end of that service Renée could do everything her pain and injury had kept her from doing. She picked up her daughters, tossed them into the air, played with them, and held them for hours. She has been pain-free ever since.

Renée now tells everyone about God's restoration of her health, family life, and vigor for ministry. Through her testimony, unbelievers have come to faith in Christ, wanderers have rededicated their lives to him, and believers have received encouragement to pursue deeper relationship with the Lord.

On December 2, 2001, the family moved to Indianapolis and began planting a new congregation. While Jeff and Renée spread the seed of vision for Crossroads Foursquare Church, they believe they will see yet more fruit glorifying God as he continues to manifest his supernatural power.

Learning to Pray With Childlike Faith

"April, I'm coming over with some ribs!"

Kathi Morse needed some adult company. Her husband, Dave, had spent all weekend working overtime at the office of his employer, the County of Santa Barbara Public Health Department, overseeing a major transition from one type of computer network to another. Late Sunday afternoon, November 11, 2001, thirty-something Kathi phoned her older sister, April Martin, to arrange dinner and conversation at the Martin home, just a few blocks away in Lompoc, California.

Along with Kathi came her daughter, Kari, seven weeks shy of age six, and three-year-old son, Aaron. April's husband, a firefighter at nearby Vandenberg Air Force Base, was on duty that day, and their two teenagers had taken off with friends. Only their son Justin, age twelve and a half, remained at home to join the backyard barbecue.

Kathi brought a family pack of boneless country-style pork ribs, and the sisters cooked two batches on the big propane grill on the patio outside the French doors. When everything was ready, they brought in the ribs and sat down to a lovely dinner.

Afterward, they decided to barbecue the leftover meat for others to enjoy later. They put the ribs on, closed the cover, and waited for them to cook.

Justin noticed first: "Hey, the grill's on fire!" By the third batch, the accumulation of dripping fat had provided ready fuel for a flare-up.

Kathi and April rushed to damp the flames and save the meat. April poured a cup of water on the fire while Kathi grabbed the tongs to move and turn the ribs so they wouldn't char. In her hurry to rescue the meat, Kathi got a bit careless. Even though she knew better, she reached across the grill and seared her hand on the superheated steam. The flames had died down, but the steam from the water caused a burn even nastier than fire would have.

Kathi cried out in pain and pulled back her hand, but not fast enough. Since she had been holding the tongs with the back of her right hand toward the grill, the tops of her outer three fingers instantly seared, turning red. The fingers began to throb and swell, and the skin became taut and shiny.

As soon as Kathi hollered, April ran inside to get a handful of cubed ice. Kathi seized a hunk and held the ice against the back of her knuckles until she could wrap a washcloth around them. Checking after ten or fifteen minutes, she was relieved to see the skin had not blistered. Still, the hair on her knuckles had completely singed off, and the swelling made the ring on her middle finger painfully tight. Kathi tried to continue visiting with her sister, but every throb of her aching hand inched up her anxiety level.

About half past seven Kathi decided that, with her husband gone, she just wanted to get her children home and prepare them for bed so she could take care of her hand. "Don't worry," she told her sister, "it's only a few blocks. I'll call you after I get the kids settled."

April, with concern in her voice, told Kathi to keep ice on her hand, get some ointment, and take aspirin. "And call me!"

Kathi collected Kari and Aaron. On the drive home, she felt sick to her stomach. Realizing that the shock of the burn was beginning to take effect, she prayed for strength just to get back safely.

Her children, worried about their mama, cooperated wonderfully. Although Kathi probably should have given them baths, she could not face the prospect of immersing her hand in warm water. So she just helped Aaron into his pajamas and put him to bed. In the process, the blanket he carried everywhere dragged across her burned knuckles. The pain from even this gentle touch almost sent her through the roof, but for Aaron's sake she stifled a yelp.

Kari took care of herself in the bathroom, brushing her teeth and putting on her jammies. Kathi's thoughts focused on getting the ice and treating her hand as her sister had urged, but she decided to finish tucking Kari into bed first. As Kathi crossed the hall from Aaron's bedroom to her daughter's room, she sensed the Holy Spirit speaking: *Have Kari pray for you.*

Her initial response to this idea did not include any particular faith for healing. *OK,* Kathi thought, *this would be a good teaching opportunity.* Kari had seen her mother intercede for others as part of the ministry team at their Nazarene church. In addition, Kathi had prayed many times with her daughter, but Mom usually led the prayer while Kari joined in and agreed. This time Kathi knew God wanted her daughter to take the lead. Still, the unacknowledged expectation in the back of her mind ran along these lines: *I'll show Kari how to pray for healing— and then I'll take care of my hand.*

Kari sat cross-legged on her bed, her long, light brown hair playing around her shoulders as she bobbed a bit, waiting for her mother. Kathi knelt beside the bed.

"Kari, I want to teach you to do something," she said. "This is what Mama does on Wednesdays and Sundays with the prayer team, when someone is sick or hurt." Kari swung her legs around and sat on the edge of the bed in front of her kneeling mom.

"I would like you to pray for me and my hand," Kathi continued, "but first ask God to tell you how to pray. Listen to what he says, and then pray just what you hear him telling you. OK?"

"OK, Mama," Kari responded. She held her mom's left hand and only the thumb of her burned right hand, and began, "Jesus, please tell me how I ought to pray for Mama."

She paused, evidently listening for the Lord's voice, as her mom had instructed. After a few seconds she started to speak, but paused to listen some more. Then she said, "God, I pray that you would heal Mama's hand, and take all the pain away." Another five or ten seconds passed. "And I pray that you would heal everybody who has burned hands." And then: "Thank you, Jesus. Amen."

Kari finished and glanced at her mom with expectation. Kathi had sensed nothing in particular during the prayer, but she noticed that her fingers did not look red any more. The ache and throbbing had stopped completely. Kathi took a deep breath and put the healing to the test, turning her hand over and drawing her knuckles across her jeans. She felt absolutely no pain.

Filled with joy, Kathi told her daughter, "Guess what, Honey? It doesn't hurt any more! Jesus healed my hand, just like you asked him to!"

"Yes! Yes! Thank you, Jesus!" Kari responded, with a smile as wide as the moon. She threw her arms around her mom and the two exchanged a long hug.

"Now here's something else you should know," Kathi continued. "When Jesus answers our prayers, we need to thank him." They spent a wonderful few moments expressing to God their grateful praise for his healing power.

Kathi also reminded her daughter, "You know, this isn't anything special we've done. We don't have to wait and call the pastor to pray. It doesn't matter if you're a child or a grown-up— we can all talk to God the same way, because the same Holy Spirit lives in us."

After Kathi tucked Kari in with the usual hug and kiss, she had opportunity to examine her hand more closely. It looked completely normal. The skin's shininess and tautness had disappeared. The swelling had gone down, and her ring no longer felt tight. The usual pink color had returned. The only difference she noticed was the lack of hair on her knuckles.

In fact, the hair on those fingers took months to grow back. Kathi thinks God, in this way, left her a reminder of what happened. Without that visual cue, the human brain can play tricks, questioning, "Did that really happen? It was all so quick, almost like a dream. Maybe the burn wasn't really so serious." For that stretch of time Kathi could show her hand as evidence when she gave this testimony.

Kathi did not forget to call her sister. Before she could speak, April wanted to know, "How are you doing? Have you taken care of your hand?"

"Are you sitting down?" Kathi asked her. She told the story, leaving April almost speechless.

Then when Dave called from work to let his wife know when he would be home, Kathi told the story again, to his amazement.

When Kathi thinks about how Jesus commended childlike faith, she realizes how much spiritual power can be released through the prayers of children. After all, childlike faith is the only kind they have. Kathi and Dave Morse just keep praying God will help them stay out of his way as their children grow in faith and boldness for life-changing ministry.

A Four-Post Walker Goes Out of Commission

Javier Echeverry's shoulders slumped when he heard his doctor's report: "He is totally disabled."

Not that his body wasn't giving him that message already. For the past fourteen and a half months, since his accident on February 15, 1996, Javier's pain had grown steadily worse. That winter day, the forty-three-year-old had slipped and fallen on a patch of ice while at his work as a welder. Instant pain had shot through his lower back and radiated down his legs, especially on the left side.

Over the next several months Javier had endured numerous X rays, MRIs, an electromyogram, a CT scan, a myelogram, and a bone scan. All had confirmed the presence of herniated and compressed discs in his spinal column, with degenerative disc disease. After physical therapy, pain medications, and injections had brought no relief, surgery had been scheduled.

On October 15, Javier had undergone a disc excision at John F. Kennedy Medical Center in Edison, New Jersey, eight miles south of his home in Plainfield. Yet his condition had slid downhill even further. When Javier had entered the hospital, he had been ambulatory—in pain, but walking on his own. When he left, he was using a four-post folding metal walker, with his suffering ratcheted up several notches.

As the years passed, Javier visited twenty-nine doctors, none of whom offered him any hope of returning to a normal, active life. Unable to put any weight on his left leg, Javier watched it begin to atrophy. His hands developed thick calluses from bearing his body on the walker, and eventually his shoulders and neck started to ache. The pain, a constant daily reality, sometimes grew so intense it gave him nausea.

This was not the life Javier had imagined when he came to the United States in 1992 from South America. He worried about whether he would be able to continue supporting his wife and three daughters in Colombia.

A diagnosis of permanent neurological impairment qualified him for state disability payments, but growing despair took its toll. Insomnia and fatigue robbed his energy and concentration. Only his faith in Jesus Christ and a new church family kept Javier from descending into a pit of hopelessness.

The First Presbyterian Church of Dunellen, about four miles southwest of Plainfield, has a history spanning about 130 years. In the early 1990s, the congregation of a few hundred members started a Spanish-speaking fellowship, Ministerio Evangelico Hispano. The fellowship grew from a handful to about fifty people under the leadership of Silvio del Campo, pastor and evangelist. Javier began attending around 1999, although his condition kept him from participating much.

The Dunellen church maintains active relationships with other congregations in the local Elizabeth Presbytery. One day Pastor Silvio got a call from his friend Lloyd Turner, a member of New Providence Presbyterian Church, a sister congregation a few miles north of Plainfield. Lloyd told him an Argentine evangelist, Sergio Scataglini, was coming to speak at Church on the Move in Allentown, Pennsylvania, about sixty miles west of Dunellen. Lloyd knew Pastor Silvio's congregation had a heart for revival.

"As you're aware," Lloyd said to his friend, "Argentina has been experiencing waves of revival for over fifteen years. Here's an opportunity for us to catch some fresh fire from God firsthand."

Folks from the two congregations made plans to carpool to Allentown. Close to a dozen members of the Dunellen Hispanic church, including Javier Echeverry, and about eight people from New Providence rode out to hear the Argentine preacher in September 2000.

Sergio spoke about the fire of God's holiness. Like many others, Javier felt the evangelist talking straight to him when he pointed at the congregation and declared, "Ninety-eight percent holiness is not enough!"

His heart stirred, Javier returned home determined to clean up his life. He began reading the Bible and attending church more regularly. As his faith deepened, he came to realize that the God of the impossible can manifest himself even in situations where humans have decreed nothing can be done. He started to believe and affirm that the Lord wanted to heal him of his crippling injury.

When Lloyd Turner learned that another Argentine, Claudio Freidzon, was coming to Church on the Move, he made sure Pastor Silvio got the information. Claudio, senior pastor of King of Kings Church in Buenos Aires, was speaking Wednesday through Friday, March 7–9, 2001.

That Wednesday Lloyd joined about fifteen members of Silvio's congregation for the road trip to Allentown. Pastor Claudio's messages on Wednesday and Thursday nights touched the Presbyterians from New Jersey so much that Silvio canceled their church's usual Friday night praise service and invited his congregation to return to Allentown for the final session of the conference.

On Friday Javier spent most of the morning in prayer. He had felt a special presence of God when he greeted Claudio Freidzon the night before, but now he sensed demonic opposition fighting to keep him from going back that evening. In the afternoon Javier read the Spanish version of Claudio's book, *Holy Spirit, I Hunger for You*. He also took note of Numbers 11:23: "The Lord answered Moses, 'Is the Lord's arm too short? You will now see whether or not what I say will come true for you.'" Javier's faith for healing quickened, and he went to that night's meeting with expectation that something wonderful was about to occur.

Pastor Claudio expressed the same expectation. His message came from 2 Kings 5, when the prophet Elisha told Naaman to wash seven times in the Jordan River to be cured of leprosy. "Tonight is your seventh dip!" Claudio proclaimed to the one thousand people gathered at Church on the Move.

After his message and prayer, Claudio invited anyone who wanted anointing or blessing to come forward for a touch through him and the ministry team. The worship band began to sing as people streamed forward. Javier, sitting in a bleacher seat close to the altar, did not hesitate. Using his walker, he maneuvered himself to the front row.

Claudio went down the line of people, briefly touching and praying for each one. When he got to Javier he placed both hands gently on his head. In just a few seconds Javier fell limply into the arms of someone behind him, who lowered him to the floor.

As Claudio moved on, Javier lay there several minutes, overcome by a sensation somewhere between dreaming and drunkenness. He attempted to get up three times without success. Ushers finally helped him to his feet. Suddenly he realized he could stand on both feet—without pain.

When he tried stepping forward, friends and others nearby who had seen his four-post walker began to cry, "Glory to God! It's a miracle!"

Claudio noticed the commotion and returned to Javier. He interrupted the worship band temporarily and asked Javier to tell what had happened.

Javier took a few tentative steps toward the front, then began walking normally. He declared, *"Dios mío!* I haven't been able to walk in five years!"

Someone passed him his folded walker, and he held it high with one hand as he ambled unaided across the room. Claudio took the walker and raised it over his head, shouting, "It's God! It's God!" The crowd roared in praise and gave a clap offering to the Lord.

For another thirty or forty-five minutes, Claudio and his team prayed for others who had come forward. Several people experienced significant healings that night. Javier, meanwhile, walked all over the sanctuary at Church on the Move, now a man on the move himself. Many witnesses to his healing wanted to greet him. Javier gave a warm bear hug to Lloyd Turner and his friends from Dunellen.

On Sunday morning, March 11, Pastor Silvio and about fifteen members of his congregation met Javier at his current home in nearby Middlesex, a mile or more from First Presbyterian of Dunellen. They decided to walk to church together as a public testimony to God's healing. Javier carried his retired walker, waving it above his shoulders.

Javier soon discovered that God had done more than heal his body. The Lord had given him zeal and effectiveness in sharing the love and power of Jesus Christ. That same Sunday afternoon Javier got a call from Colombia, telling him his sister had suffered a heart attack. Yet the next day, as he interceded for her, he experienced what he interpreted as a divine manifestation. An unusual breeze swept through his room, even though the door and windows were closed. He sensed God declaring his sister's healing.

On Wednesday when Javier called his family in Colombia, they confirmed it: His sister, also a believer, was now healed. Doctors canceled plans to operate on her coronary arteries.

Javier began an active evangelistic outreach to nearby Spanish-speaking neighborhoods. He walked the streets sharing his testimony, passed out tracts, ministered in hospitals, and led many to the Lord.

Silvio del Campo and his church had been praying for revival for some time, and Javier's healing seemed to ignite a mightier move of the Holy Spirit. The congregation, which had plateaued at about fifty people for the past couple of years, grew to seventy, eighty, then ninety within a few months.

That summer the Dunellen church sponsored an open-air rally in Washington Square for their local community. Hundreds who came and enjoyed free food and music also heard Pastor Silvio and Javier testify to his miraculous healing and saw him dance with joy in worship of the Lord. Almost five thousand more heard the story in July, when Lloyd Turner and a small team from his church in New Providence traveled to Argentina and told Claudio Freidzon and the King of Kings congregation about the tremendous impact of his ministry through the healing of this one man.

Javier and others have learned many faith lessons from his healing, including the importance of persistence in prayer, holiness, obedience, and patient trust despite years of waiting. God chose to delay Javier's healing until one thousand witnesses could praise him for it.

Lloyd Turner, for one, believes his spiritual life has changed forever since observing firsthand this display of God's power. "I feel the Lord has given me a giant wake-up call to be bolder about sharing my faith and praying for revival," he says. "I have been encouraged to share this message of hope with friends and relatives who seek spiritual and physical wholeness through our Lord Jesus Christ." The message continues to spread, to the glory of God.

The Agony of the Feet

This can't be happening!

Sharon Trainor was beside herself. *How can this pain be back, after the operations cut my nerves?* Her mind churned with rising panic. *Surgery was successful! Doctors told me I would never have a problem again! What does this mean?*

Her doctors had no answers. "This shouldn't have happened. We haven't seen a case like this, where the pain returned."

Sharon knew her doctors had not seen many cases of her disease to begin with. The original diagnosis of Reflex Sympathetic Dystrophy Syndrome (RSDS, also known as RSD) in the early fall of 1991 came after four months of tests and evaluations that could not pinpoint what was wrong. A sore, aching right foot swelled up, and within a week turned purple and ice-cold. Any touch—even a sheet—on Sharon's foot caused excruciating pain.

Steroids and pain medication did nothing to ease the agony that got so intense Sharon sometimes had to go to the nearest hospital's Emergency Department for a shot of morphine. She tried outpatient injections of nerve blocks straight into the spine. They helped for a day or two before the burning pain flared up worse than ever.

A vascular surgeon then suggested a sympathectomy. The sympathetic nervous system regulates blood flow to the skin, and the surgery would sever the nerves in Sharon's lower spine that controlled this system in her right leg. "There's only a 50 percent chance of success," he said, "but if it works it should give you complete relief."

It worked. The pain and swelling vanished, and her foot's

color and temperature returned to normal. The operation that fall also disabled Sharon's oil and perspiration glands below the waist on that side, but she considered such loss a negligible price to pay for regaining a life free of physical torment.

Sharon had already faced suffering and adversity of other kinds. A child-abuse survivor and daughter of alcoholics, Sharon had been raising three children as a single mom when RSDS first hit. After the surgery enabled her to return to work, she deepened her relationship with the man who had supported her through that difficult period. In June 1994, at age thirty-seven, Sharon married John Trainor, ten years her junior. They bought a house in King of Prussia, Pennsylvania, fifteen miles northwest of Philadelphia.

In March 1996, however, RSDS reemerged in Sharon's left foot. This time she refused steroids because of their side effects. Nerve blocks enabled her to sleep but wore off so quickly she had to return every few days for another. Before long she convinced her doctor to try a second sympathectomy. "It worked for my right foot," she reasoned. "Why wait?"

Again the surgery brought instant relief. Yet by the early spring of 1999 the unthinkable had happened: Pain flared afresh, first in Sharon's right foot and soon in her left.

Sharon had started researching her disease, and what she learned frightened her. Doctors still know little about the cause of RSDS. In recent years most have concluded that sympathectomies, despite the immediate respite, only set up the patient for worse pain later. In many cases RSDS eventually attacks all of the body's organs. Sharon discovered that from the time of diagnosis a patient's remaining life span may be shortened to as few as ten years.

Sharon began seeing a neurologist at Thomas Jefferson University Hospital in Philadelphia, but soon became too disabled to work and had to use a wheelchair. Periodically she entered the hospital for a week-long dose of morphine administered through a catheter in her spine. At first this helped enough to get her out of the wheelchair and using a walker for almost six weeks at a time. Yet as the treatments' effectiveness ebbed, she had to return to the wheelchair after only two weeks or so.

Sharon grieved that she could no longer fulfill her roles as wife and mother to her three teenagers. She began feeling an urge to pray for her family, for God to take care of them. Both she and John had Catholic backgrounds, but had not been walking with the Lord. During Sharon's pain-free stretches after the surgeries, they had partied weekly at the local tavern. After Sharon became hospitalized, John had hit the bar by himself.

While the family attended the Catholic church for Christmas and Easter, John had actually become a confirmed atheist. As Sharon's illness progressed and she started seeking the Lord more, she asked her husband to take the children to church, since she could not go. From time to time the four of them dutifully left for an hour on Sunday morning, but Sharon learned much later that they often skipped out on church in favor of Dunkin' Donuts.

A few times during 1999 Sharon's friend Jayne Rodden let her know about healing services in the area, and John took her. Yet Sharon realized that her continued disability only served to harden her husband's attitude: *There is no God, because he is not answering her prayers.*

Once or twice Sharon visited Jayne's fellowship, Harvest Rock Church in Havertown, just west of Philadelphia. Although she enjoyed it, she could not imagine John attending. Her heart was especially touched when the pastors, Jack and Jane Hanley, called on her at Jefferson Hospital twice, although they barely knew her.

On Thursday, December 9, 1999, Sharon entered the hospital with symptoms of a stroke: slurred speech, sagging mouth, jumbled thinking. After tests, however, doctors determined the problem was actually a toxic level of all the medications she was taking.

Around eleven o'clock one night Sharon lay in her hospital

bed and cried out to God: *What can I learn from this?* She felt numb and confused.

Quickly a supernatural, unexplainable joy rose in her heart and filled her body. The Lord gave her a word of knowledge, revealing that she would be the vessel by which her family would come to know him. Even though Sharon herself had not yet entered a personal relationship with Jesus, she knew this connection was important. Although she could not fathom how God would get through to her family, he gave her peace to trust him to do it.

She could barely contain her happiness. So much energy surged through her that she wanted to jump up and down. She phoned her husband, bubbling with the news. "John, everything is going to be OK! I mean everything!"

"I know it will be, Honey," John answered. Yet Sharon could hear the skepticism in his voice, and she did not try to explain what she meant by "everything." She knew he probably thought she was doped from the drugs, but just kept repeating her declaration until John responded with more enthusiasm. She herself had no doubt—God had spoken.

Just after the doctors detoxified Sharon's system, she returned to the hospital for a previously scheduled spinal infusion to block the pain to her feet for another week or two. On December 18, she came home.

The timing could not have worked better. Sharon had asked her family to attend a special Christmas service at Harvest Rock Church on Sunday the nineteenth, figuring this might be a good way to introduce them to the congregation. Fresh from her morphine treatment, she would be able to get around using her walker rather than the wheelchair. The family agreed to make this their Christmas church event that year.

The service at Harvest Rock featured a live nativity drama with the "Hearts of Worship" team, special guests that Sunday. Even John seemed to enjoy it. Toward the end a member of the worship team pointed to Sharon with a brief prophetic message:

"God has big plans for you." She remembered what God had said about using her to reach her family, and when the invitation came to receive Jesus Christ as personal Savior, Sharon headed straight for the altar to surrender her life to him.

Sharon sensed a softening in John's heart. At a friend's house that month he had spied a book on her coffee table entitled *The Case for Christ*. He expressed his interest to their daughter Colleen, and she bought him a copy for Christmas. That holiday season Sharon felt especially blessed to celebrate Christ's birth with her family. Now in her ninth year of RSDS, she wondered if she would share any more Christmases with them.

By January Sharon had lost confidence in the doctor prescribing her medication. After her toxic episode, she could not face the idea that the only response to her worsening condition was more drugs. John got a referral for a new neurologist, and on Monday, January 24, 2000, Sharon went to see him at Hahnemann University Hospital in Philadelphia. Dr. Jahangir Maleki gave her hope he could wean her off the drugs and try a different approach to dealing with the pain of RSDS.

That evening, Harvest Rock Church in Havertown held a special healing service with guest speaker Ché Ahn, senior pastor of Harvest Rock Church in Pasadena, California, and founder of Harvest International Ministries. Jayne Rodden made sure Sharon heard about it, and she attended with John. Because of a recent morphine infusion, she again brought only her walker.

The church was packed with perhaps two hundred people. After a brief gospel message, Pastor Ché then gave an altar call for those who wanted to renew their faith or receive Jesus for the first time. Sharon decided to make a fresh commitment. When she got to the front, she found—to her astonished joy—John right behind her. He surrendered his heart to Jesus that night.

After people returned to the pews, Pastor Ché said he had received some words of knowledge about conditions the Lord wanted to heal that night. He prayed for the Holy Spirit to touch the congregation corporately with healing. Some gave testimonies about instant changes in their bodies. Yet Sharon did not feel any better. Ché invited anyone who still wanted prayer to assemble downstairs in the fellowship hall after the service so he could minister personally. He instructed those who had responded to the altar call to stand in the first row.

When the service closed, John carried Sharon downstairs. Perhaps a third of the congregation stayed afterward along with them. Pastor Ché began moving down the front row, praying briefly and sometimes laying his hands on people. With the number waiting, he did not ask for prayer requests but seemed to pray according to divine leading. Sharon knew that even if he did not notice her walker, her slippers might clue him that she had a problem with her feet. Although she could not bear anything to touch them, in winter she could not go without protection. So when she went out she wore oversized, puffy, pink terry slippers with open backs so her feet could slide in.

John stood behind Sharon. When Ché got to her, he started to pray but stopped. "I'm sensing a resistance," he said, "something blocking you from being able to receive. Do you have any problems with shame, guilt, unworthiness?"

Sharon said yes to all three, recalling the trauma of her childhood. Pastor Ché rebuked these from her body in the name of Jesus and broke a generational curse over her life. In a moment Sharon started weeping. She felt a sensation like a rush of wind blowing through her, and suddenly found herself on the floor. John caught her just before she hit.

Ché bent down and grabbed her slippers. "Your faith has healed you," he said. "How do you feel?"

"Scared!" Sharon replied.

As Pastor Ché went on to the next person in line, Sharon felt her feet begin to tremble. The uncontrollable shaking moved up her legs. She thought she must be cold, but couldn't feel anything. A warm shiver then ran up her spine to her head, and in that instant she realized she had no more pain.

For several minutes she lay quietly, savoring the relief. She feared if she moved or said anything, the pangs might return. Eventually she turned to John, sitting next to her in his own shocked silence. "John! My pain is gone!"

"What? Are you kidding?"

Sharon had her husband help her sit up. "I want to know how I got down here on the floor. Ché Ahn must have blown me backward—that's just what it felt like."

"Sharon, he didn't touch you," John replied. "He didn't do anything like that."

The dumbfounded couple sat on the floor for perhaps forty-five minutes while everyone else received prayer. The room began to empty. Pastor Jack Hanley finally came over and said, "We're going to have to close up now."

Reluctantly, Sharon let John assist her to her feet. She still felt as though anything she did might break the spell and bring the pain rushing back. She took a step without her walker. Then another, and another. No pain. She crossed the room to the stairs, then looked back. John, wide-eyed, watching, had not moved.

"C'mere, John!" Sharon called. "You know I can't do these steps!"

Yet she did, without his help. The awe lingered on the way home as they drove in silence, wondering how long this miracle would last.

The next morning Sharon got up to use the bathroom and realized the pain had not returned. Yet she crawled right back into bed, still in fear that it would.

John, however, was bursting with joy. A heavy snowstorm had passed through overnight, preventing him from leaving for work. With energy to burn, he began shoveling sidewalks. When he came back in, he asked Sharon, "Where's that church? I should go over there and shovel the parking lot!"

Sharon could not believe the transformation in her husband. He called the church and told Pastor Jack what had happened. Jack said he would phone and tell Ché Ahn. Ché had stayed with the Hanleys overnight, but they had arranged for a four-wheel-drive vehicle to take him to his next engagement in Harrisburg, almost one hundred miles west.

Meanwhile, Sharon herself spent three days in bed, unwilling to risk disturbing her pain relief. About four or five o'clock Friday morning, however, she woke from sleep with the same overwhelming joy she had felt in the hospital in December, when God had assured her about her family's salvation—the same joy John now displayed. From that moment, she knew without doubt she had been healed. She got up, put on some worship music, and began baking cookies.

Now the Trainors could not stop praising God. They cleaned their home of spiritually questionable items. John stopped drinking, cold turkey.

Their children, while delighted at their mom's newfound mobility, were confused and suspicious about the radical changes in their parents. Colleen, a sophomore at George Washington University in Washington, D.C., lived on campus, while Sean, a senior in high school, spent little time at home because of his sports involvement. So Heather, a freshman in high school, felt the biggest impact. With a handful of other teens from Harvest Rock, her parents took her to the large youth ministry meetings at Newark Christian Fellowship down the river in Delaware.

Heather often phoned her sister with updates on the home situation, and Colleen wondered what kind of cult her parents might have her in. When she returned home for spring break, she went with Heather one Sunday night to investigate the youth meetings. The love of Jesus blindsided her, and she came out saved. Heather herself waited until August to give her life to Christ, on the bus ride back from a Young Life camp. Then in September, the day before Sean left to enter Ohio State University in Columbus, he prayed the sinner's prayer with his mom. A week later God connected him with both the campus Christian fellowship and a local church.

Within nine months the Lord had fulfilled his promise to Sharon.

At the same time, he did a complete makeover on her body. By the end of March she had weaned herself off all painkillers. The Lord also healed her of a long-standing reading disability. That fall tests showed her glaucoma had disappeared. In December she discontinued medication for a thyroid condition, and three months later her doctor confirmed that healing.

When Sharon phoned Dr. Maleki in the spring of 2000 to tell him she had been healed of RSDS, he asked her to tell her story at a pain conference for fifteen or twenty other neurologists and pain control specialists, held at Hahnemann Hospital. Dr. Maleki gave the physicians the entire history of Sharon's illness, with slides of her tests and other documentation. Then he had her stand and recount what had happened. Dr. Maleki also invited her to visit and encourage his other RSDS patients.

The Hanleys urged John and Sharon to travel to Ontario, Canada, for a spring conference at the Toronto Airport Christian Fellowship. Ché Ahn, one of the speakers, asked if Sharon would be willing to share her testimony. Since then she has told the story of God's healing power at several other churches and settings, and on Christian radio.

Moreover, God has given Sharon and John a ministry of praying for the sick. They have seen several people healed by the power of the Holy Spirit, with some amazing miracles. They are also growing in prophetic gifting. Sharon often gets dreams and visions, and John receives words of knowledge, which work together to direct them how to pray for people.

The Trainors' lives have changed so drastically, in every aspect, that they can hardly believe they are the same people. Indeed, they are not. John has tried to explain everything that happened this way: "It was not a healing of the mind, but the orchestration of a loving metamorphosis in the life of a family. God made all this occur, with all this detail, because he loves us totally and wanted us to know he was present in our daily lives."

FOUR

Dreams, Visions, and Angel Encounters

FROM ANCIENT TIMES, people of all cultures have received supernatural revelation from dreams and visions. Such channels have yielded everything from individual nuggets of guidance to the establishment of new world religions. Clearly dreams, visions, trances, and visitations provide a powerful avenue for the spiritual realm to connect with the natural realm. Yet here, even more than with other signs and wonders, we need correct discernment of the source of these experiences to avoid demonic deception.

Visions and visitations, sometimes of angels or other spirit beings, can come to people who are open-eyed and fully awake. In the case of dreams and night visions, our sleeping souls may provide easier access for spiritual communication than when our analytical minds are in charge. Both God and Satan can use this receptivity to their advantage, as the Bible illustrates. Alternatively, we may receive images generated by nothing more than the human subconscious or psychotropic drugs—or even last night's pizza.

Believers do well to pray regularly for protection against deceiving spirits, for discernment of the source of revelation received in these ways, and for proper interpretation of messages coming from God.

Even the truth of the revelation does not provide conclusive evidence of its divine origin. Psychics, for instance, may sometimes see accurately via the supernatural realm, but their knowledge comes not from God but from occult and demonic imposters. While many reports have surfaced of Christians who dreamed beforehand about the terrorist attacks of September 11, 2001, some of Osama bin Laden's colleagues also received prior dreams and visions about planes flying into buildings.

Nonetheless, believers who trust in God's greater power to protect them from deception need not fear inviting him to communicate in this way. As with other signs and wonders, examination of the event's effects provides one of the best ways to evaluate the supernatural source. All divinely initiated signs will glorify God and the Lord Jesus Christ in some manner. In addition, dreams and related phenomena that come from God will bear good fruit somehow, providing godly guidance, encouragement to deeper faith or holiness, evidence of his love, or reassurance of his control over a situation. Prophetic revelation received by such means and shared according to the Lord's direction may break through barriers of resistance to the gospel and bring people to faith in Christ, the best fruit of all.

Is It God Speaking, or the Chocolate?

The morning sun streamed through the bedroom window as Cheryl Irvine awoke about a quarter past seven on Thursday, August 9, 2001. She heard her husband, a family practice physician, hurrying to get ready to leave their house in Loma Rica, California. Bill was on call that morning and needed to drive to the Emergency Department (E.D.) to admit a patient before returning for his regular appointments beginning at 9:00. Their rural community, nestled in the foothills of the Sierra Nevada some fifty miles north of Sacramento, lay half an hour from the nearest E.D. Cheryl knew Bill had little time to spare.

Still, something compelled her to share a vivid dream that had come overnight. She gave her husband a condensed version while he finished preparing to leave.

"Well, that's pretty outlandish," Bill responded good-naturedly, when he heard the tale. "Are you sure you didn't eat too much chocolate last night?"

They both laughed. Yet Cheryl could not shake the dream from her memory. After Bill left, the forty-two-year-old wife and home-schooling mother of seven children played back the scenes in her mind.

At the beginning of the dream, Cheryl found herself looking out a picture window that stretched from floor to ceiling on the landing of a staircase. A beautiful architectural masterpiece dominated the panorama outside. Sensing an unseen companion just behind and to her right, Cheryl commented, "We are so blessed to have a view of this world-famous tower from here where we're staying." She felt as though she were on a trip with a professional tour guide.

As the dream continued, Cheryl and her companion went to the window at various times during their stay to gaze at the tower and the harbor beyond it. They admired the tower's beauty, especially at night, when it glowed with thousands of lights. It reached so high Cheryl had to lean her head all the way back to see the top.

Her companion never came into her field of view, and Cheryl never turned to look because she focused outside the window at things being presented to her. Yet she felt especially comfortable with this person.

Then one morning Cheryl clambered to the window again to enjoy the scene, but all had changed. To her horror, smoke billowed from the top of the tower. Large commercial airplanes flew chaotically through the sky, level with the upper portion of the tower. Cheryl saw ships on alert in the harbor, while the scream of sirens filled the air.

Her heart pounded as her mind struggled to comprehend. "What happened?" she gasped.

Cheryl sensed her unseen companion approach quietly and stop just behind her right shoulder. She heard a concise response: "Terrorists have attacked the tower, and now there is a war."

Suddenly Cheryl felt a deep awareness that her calm companion was the Lord Jesus. In anguish and astonishment over his news, she cried, "No, Lord! Not in America! A war over a tower? Please, Lord, don't let it happen!"

At the same moment, Cheryl, still dreaming, realized she was dreaming. She asked God to make the dream start over and prevent the horror from taking place. "Please, Lord, let everything be all right again!"

The scene changed. Once again Cheryl stood before a picture window. She saw a beautiful tower, standing tall and intact against the orange sky of a sunrise or sunset. Joy and relief welled up as she concluded God had answered her prayer: The dream had started over and the attack had not occurred.

At the same time, Cheryl noticed she did not have to lean her head all the way back to see the top of this tower. It appeared slightly nearer to her. Yet she minimized these differences in her hopeful conclusion that God had rewound the tape and erased the tragedy.

Then the voice of her unseen companion came again: "Look closer."

All of a sudden Cheryl's view zoomed in on the tower as though coming through the lens of a powerful telescope. On the building's side she observed intricate iron scrollwork not present on the original tower. With its ornate decoration and artwork, she realized she was seeing a new and even more beautiful tower.

Cheryl rejoiced that the rest of the scene remained peaceful—the sky free of airplanes, ships quiet in the harbor, no sirens piercing the air.

At that point Cheryl woke up. In the darkness she thanked God that this intense experience had been only a dream and the horrible events had not really taken place. Comforting herself with these thoughts, she drifted back to sleep.

After sharing her dream with her husband, Cheryl wondered if God might be giving a message through it. Yet the dream scenes so overwhelmed her, she pushed thoughts of them to the back of her mind and did not inquire of the Lord any further concerning their content or meaning.

Weeks passed. In addition to Cheryl's responsibilities for home and family, she stayed busy with her usual activities at Loma Rica Community Church, an interdenominational congregation with an emphasis on worship, personal growth, and outreach. Cheryl ministered on the worship team, while her husband served as an elder. Together they led a discipleship group for teenagers, meeting weekly in their home.

Then came Monday, September 10. As Cheryl did housework, a recurring thought plagued her that "something big and really bad" was going to happen the next day. By 11:30 P.M. she felt God directing her to pray and read the Bible.

With her family asleep, Cheryl entered her walk-in closet, where she could turn on a light without disturbing anyone. An intense heaviness and grief overcame her as she knelt in God's presence. She wept and pleaded for God's mercy, not knowing what she was interceding about. Quickly she reviewed the needs of various friends and family members, but none seemed appropriate to prompt such urgency.

"What's going on, Lord?" she asked. The only answer was an increased burden to pray in the Spirit.

Cheryl glanced down at the pages of her Bible, opened randomly on the floor in front of her. Her eyes fell on Lamentations 3:21-26 (KJV): "This I recall to my mind, therefore I have hope. It is because of the Lord's mercies that we are not consumed, because his compassions fail not. They are new every morning: great is thy faithfulness. The Lord is my portion, saith my soul; therefore will I hope in him. The Lord is good unto them that wait for him, to the soul that seeketh him. It is good that a man should both hope and quietly wait for the salvation of the Lord."

She prayed in response, "Yes, Lord; it is by your mercies that we are not consumed, so great are our sins." She thanked God for his unfailing love and faithfulness, and spent a few minutes looking up more verses about mercy. Around midnight she felt a release from intercessory prayer and went to bed.

About seven o'clock Tuesday morning, Cheryl had just finished dressing and was brushing her teeth when her husband came into the bathroom holding their youngest daughter, not quite two.

"Cheryl, I don't mean to frighten you," Bill said, "but something very bad has just happened to our country. Planes have crashed into the World Trade Center and the Pentagon."

"What?" Cheryl exclaimed. "How could that happen? What's going on?" Her thoughts first ran to some terrible coincidence of accidents. She hurried downstairs to watch the television news, staring with Bill at the mind-numbing scenes on their screen.

As Cheryl gathered her wits about her, she recalled Monday's sense of impending calamity, and her intense intercession of the previous night. She told Bill about how God had alerted her to pray. Then the memory of her dream of August 9 tiptoed back into her mind.

"Terrorists have attacked the tower, and now there is a war." The words of Cheryl's unseen dream companion echoed over and over. Now as never before, Cheryl sought the Lord about whether her dream had come from him. Despite the similarities, she did not want to presume without asking for confirmation.

Over the next two days, Cheryl went through stages of travailing in prayer, with fears for her children's future, to a quiet faith that God was still in control. By Thursday evening, September 13—Cheryl's birthday—as she continued asking the Lord for discernment about her dream, she felt led to open her husband's Bible. Her eyes were drawn to Amos 3:6-7: "When a trumpet sounds in a city, do not the people tremble? When disaster comes to a city, has not the Lord caused it? Surely the Sovereign Lord does nothing without revealing his plan to his servants the prophets."

Eventually Cheryl concluded—through these Scriptures, her own prayer, and the counsel of her husband and others—that the dream of August, the warnings of Monday, and the profound intercessory prayer session all represented workings of the Holy Spirit in her life. The Lord assured her of his love, his guidance, and his ability to speak to her.

President George W. Bush called for a National Day of Prayer and Mourning on Friday, September 14. After watching the televised service held at Washington National Cathedral, Cheryl took some of her children to Loma Rica Community Church for a home-school play group. Pastor Wayne Vincent arrived about half past eleven to prepare for their noon community prayer gathering. Cheryl felt led to tell him of her experiences. He listened intently, and invited her to share during the service.

Afterward, many people expressed their gratitude. Cheryl's dream brought a measure of comfort that the Lord knew in advance what would happen. The story encouraged those who heard it to build their faith that God is in control.

Cheryl herself now experiences a heightened sense of discernment about when God is speaking to her. She has greater trust that her prayers of intercession, prompted by the Lord, are making a difference. Her dream has inspired a deeper desire to seek holiness and a closer relationship with God. Also, her worship and awe of her heavenly Father have grown as she sees his grace abounding in the midst of evil.

"By their fruit you will recognize them," Jesus said in Matthew 7:16. The fruit of Cheryl's dream has brought unmistakable glory to God, and she gives him all the praise for his wondrous works.

September 11—in July

One night around the end of July 2001, seventeen-year-old Amanda Rae Trott woke in the wee hours with a disturbing dream. The nightmarish images replayed in her mind until her racing heart calmed and she fell back to sleep. In the morning, however, the scenes returned to memory so fresh and real she felt as though she had lived them. Because Mandi did not often recall her dreams, the intensity of this one caused her to reflect and pray about its source and meaning.

Mandi's church background provided little instruction in dream interpretation. With her father in the Marine Corps, her family moved frequently, and she attended mostly Baptist churches in whatever city she found herself. Her dad was stat-ioned in New Orleans, Louisiana, as a gunnery sergeant when Mandi finished her secondary schooling in May 2001, so she received her high school diploma from Belle Chasse High in Cajun country.

Since Mandi had accepted Christ as Savior at age seven, her relationship with the Lord had grown steadily, but especially during the past couple of years in New Orleans she had experienced awesome new depths of spirituality. The youth group at First Baptist Church of Belle Chasse held Bible studies every Tuesday night, and she had begun to understand prayer as a two-way conversation rather than a monologue of petitions.

In addition, her father's sister provided a source of spiritual stability to which Mandi turned regularly. As a woman of faith, Aunt Lisa served as a mentor to Mandi, who phoned whenever she wanted to talk or ask questions. Lisa's husband, Michael French, was president of Advocate Ministries in Birmingham, Alabama, with a focus on deliverance and prophetic ministry.

Still, amid preparations for college that summer, Mandi wrestled in bewilderment with the dreadful dream scenes that had commandeered her thoughts that one night.

The dream began with a prayer circle. Twenty or thirty people knelt together, holding hands, with heads bowed. Mandi and most of the others were crying. She had a strong sense that America was under attack by another country, with the inter-cessors' location in danger.

As she looked up during prayer, Mandi noticed the group's surroundings: a large office with cubicles and computers. She had a sense of familiarity, as though she came here daily.

The view from the windows, nearly floor to ceiling, told Mandi they were in a high-rise building. Two other buildings stood close by, so tall she could not see the tops from where she knelt. Towering above the rest of the urban scene outside, these buildings shared similar dimensions, but the one on Mandi's right seemed a little closer.

Just then a large commercial jetliner roared into view from the left and struck the nearer of the two towers. The intercessors screamed as black smoke billowed around the stricken building.

After a minute of chaos, the group resumed crying out to God with even greater intensity. Then a moment later another plane flew at full bore into the second tower. More screams arose, but even more quickly this time the intercessors bowed their heads and returned to prayer. Mandi felt grateful that their own building had not been hit.

In an instant the scene changed dramatically. Mandi found herself outside at night on a military base, with a tall chain-link fence surrounding the compound. Half a dozen guards dressed in green camouflage loitered nearby with M-16 rifles slung over their shoulders. To Mandi the guards looked like foreigners with dark skin, and she realized that she was imprisoned in their camp.

At a gate in the fence, several eighteen-wheel trucks with headlights burning had come to deliver supplies. Guards motioned them in, while other big rigs that had dropped their loads prepared to leave. Mandi saw her opportunity to escape. She sneaked up next to an eighteen-wheeler, on the side opposite the guards, as the truck slowly approached the gate. She hoped the box trailer would shield her from view until she got outside the fenced compound.

However, the truck stopped, and one of the guards strode around the front and spied Mandi. He lowered his rifle and shouted at her in an unfamiliar language, yet she understood his meaning precisely. She got the sense she had made previous escape attempts and this guard had caught her before. Her painful frustration lingered as the dream ended.

Mandi stewed about her dream all day. It seemed significant, but she had no idea what it could mean. The feeling that the United States was being attacked by another country did not seem to match the images of planes crashing into buildings. That evening, she related the dream to the college minister at her Tuesday Bible study, but he offered no suggestions on how to respond. Mandi wondered if he thought the whole experience a bit strange.

The next day she phoned her aunt, hoping for more encouragement.

"Mandi, you should write down your dream," Aunt Lisa advised her. "I can't tell you what it means, but it's quite interesting. Pray about it and write it down. Maybe the Lord will show you the meaning later."

Mandi prayed about it, but did not take the time to write. She began to think, *Maybe it really was just a crazy dream.*

In August Mandi moved to Birmingham, Alabama, leaving her two younger sisters and younger brother at home with their parents in New Orleans. Mandi enrolled at Jefferson State Community College, staying with her aunt Donna Faulkner, another of her father's sisters.

Just about eight o'clock on Tuesday morning, September 11, Aunt Donna, still in her nightclothes, came into Mandi's room to wake her with fragmented news. "Mandi, something just happened to the World Trade Center in New York. A plane hit it, or something."

Mandi turned on the television in her room and sat agog at the unbelievable images of terror. When the second airplane struck Tower 2, she began to bawl. Amid the commentators' talk of the "attack on America," all she could think about was her father in the Marine Corps. For hours she wrestled with feelings of fear and devastation. She even wondered, "Why is this so emotional for me? Yeah, Dad's in the military, but that doesn't really explain what I'm going through."

Then her summer dream slipped back into her consciousness.

Recalling the scenes—and how they had just come to life before her on the television screen—felt like a blow to the head.

Mandi went to tell her Aunt Donna. When Aunt Donna heard that her niece had called Lisa French after the dream, she urged Mandi to contact her again.

That evening Mandi phoned. "Aunt Lisa, do you remember that dream I had?" Mandi heard a gasp as her aunt, too, suddenly put it together. They noted that God must have known all along what would happen, and perhaps gave Mandi the dream to reassure her of his ultimate control. The dream's emphasis on intercession also spoke of the responsibility of believers to pray whenever God gives a specific burden.

Not until later did Mandi learn about the eight aid workers with Shelter Now who had been imprisoned in Afghanistan in early August under charges of illegally preaching Christianity. As the media focused on the two young American women, especially after bombing of Afghanistan began in October in response to the terrorist attacks, Mandi wondered if the second part of her dream reflected their plight. She kept them in constant prayer until their safe release in November.

That fall Mandi moved in with Michael and Lisa French and began attending Cahaba Christian Fellowship in Birmingham, pastored by her uncle Michael. The Lord continued teaching her about the many ways he speaks to his people today. She sensed him saying, *Look at how much I know about the world. While you're asleep, things are going on that I am fully aware of. No matter what, I am still in control, day and night.*

Mandi now pays attention whenever she has a memorable dream, asking God if he is giving her a message through it. She has no doubt God communicates not only through dreams but in all kinds of ways—"even to me, a teenager."

Supernaturally Transported to Prison
The Church at NorthGate was packed. During the special guest conference from August 14–17, 2001, people hungry for more

of the Lord filled the one-thousand-seat auditorium of this church near Woodstock, Georgia, north of Atlanta on the Interstate 575 corridor. Todd Bentley, a twenty-five-year-old evangelist from British Columbia, taught about the Holy Spirit's current impartation of spiritual gifts throughout the body of Christ. He relayed many words of knowledge about conditions the Lord wanted to heal: deafness, heart ailments, chronic fatigue syndrome, arthritis. Dozens of people received healing, deliverance, or other supernatural manifestations of the touch of God.

Todd had seen this kind of spiritual outpouring countless times before. Since his dramatic conversion at age eighteen from a life of drugs and debauchery, the Spirit of God had given him an awesome anointing for signs and wonders, particularly healing. He began to receive invitations to minister, first locally and soon internationally, teaching the Word of God and building people's faith for a greater revelation of God's kingdom in all its fullness. Thousands had put their trust in Christ after hearing the gospel and seeing it demonstrated in power under Todd's Fresh Fire Ministries.

Friday evening, August 17, at the Church at NorthGate began in typical fashion. As he often does, Todd went to the back of the worship center before the meeting and sat in the last pew to wait on the Lord, seeking insight about what God might want to do that night. Todd desires to minister as Jesus did when he said, "The Son can do nothing by himself; he can do only what he sees his Father doing, because whatever the Father does the Son also does" (Jn 5:19).

Suddenly Todd found himself somewhere else. Anyone in the church would have seen his body still sitting at the back of the room, but in his spirit Todd had an experience like that of Ezekiel when the Spirit of God lifted him up and took him to Jerusalem from his home in Babylonian exile (see Ez 8).

Todd's trance put him on Interstate 75, driving north from Atlanta. As he came to an overpass he saw a sign announcing his approach to Chattanooga. Although Todd knew little about the geography of the area, he learned later that this city lay just across the northern border of Georgia in Tennessee.

He ended up at a prison. There he was taken inside and led to a young man wearing glasses. Todd knew in his spirit that this man was in his early twenties, had recently come to faith in Christ, and was imprisoned for crimes committed before his conversion.

Todd had a word from the Lord to deliver to the young inmate. God revealed he was going to give him an evangelistic ministry, empowered by miracles, signs, and wonders. God also wanted to reassure him he was on the Lord's heart and mind, even in prison.

As soon as Todd shared this message with the young man, his trance ended and he found himself back in the last pew of the Church at NorthGate.

Todd sensed that this vision would mean something to someone attending that night. Later, during the service, as Todd called out various words of knowledge, he recounted this story from the platform. Suddenly a woman jumped to her feet and cried, "That's my friend's son!" She came forward and said, "My friend wanted to come to the meeting tonight but couldn't make it because of things going on at home. She has a boy in prison."

This woman, flushed with excitement, pulled out her cell phone and called her friend on the spot. When she answered, the woman handed the phone to Todd. The young man's mother confirmed everything Todd had seen in his vision: The interstate goes north from Atlanta to the Chattanooga prison; her son was twenty-two years old and wore glasses; and he had committed his crimes before his recent conversion to Christ while imprisoned.

Todd repeated to the mother his word from the Lord for her son. Moreover, the Holy Spirit gave him additional words of knowledge during the conversation, revealing the presence of witchcraft in the home. He prayed and took authority over this evil, rebuking Satan's attack on the family.

The mother, almost speechless with astonishment, told Todd her seventeen-year-old son, still living at home, was involved in Satanism and had tried to kill his father that very evening. Todd's phone conversation and prayer, she said, seemed to have defused the situation.

The conversation ended, but the night was not over. A short while later, the young man's mother arrived at the meeting. The crisis at her home had calmed so completely that she was able to leave and drive to the Church at NorthGate to see Todd in person. The congregation rejoiced to hear how God had ministered to this needy family through supernatural signs confirming his love and protection of them.

Todd has every expectation that someday he will receive a report about the twenty-two-year-old son's ministry of evangelism, accompanied by signs and wonders.

An Angel Named Revival

Visions and trances have also become a recurring part of Todd Bentley's experience. Sometimes God allows him to see angels.

On Saturday, February 17, 2001, Todd was ministering at the Albany Vineyard Christian Fellowship in Albany, Oregon, about seventy miles south of Portland. He had visited extensively there over the previous couple of months as the Holy Spirit poured out healing and revival, with more than 150 people making first-time decisions to trust Christ. That night during worship the Lord gave him an open-eyed vision.

Todd looked toward the pulpit and saw a tall angel towering toward the ceiling of the church. The young-looking figure had blond hair, close to shoulder length, in a bob cut. Wearing a white robe with a yellow sash, the angel glowed with awesome brightness.

As Todd gazed at this radiant form he heard God speak with an inner voice. The Lord told him the angel's name was Revival. He said this spirit ranked underneath the archangels in the heavenly hierarchy, meaning the angel did not have authority to confront principalities over nations but could deal with powers over cities. Moreover, God explained that this angel had a commission to bring revival to cities through outpourings of divine healing.

Todd remembered the story from John 5:1-9 about the angel who came periodically to stir the pool of Bethesda, bringing God's blessing to heal the first person who got into the water after it moved. He came to understand that the angel he saw at the Albany Vineyard had a similar assignment to open "wells" of healing—portals through which the power of the Great Physician would flow freely.

As Todd marveled at his vision, God spoke again. *Go ask that woman standing across the room what she's seeing. She'll confirm what I've just shown you.*

Todd went over to the woman God had pointed out, a twenty-six-year-old pastor's daughter from Grants Pass, Oregon. She told him she could see a huge angel standing at the pulpit. Her description matched the one in Todd's vision.

With the Holy Spirit's presence hovering powerfully in the room, Todd realized as the meeting progressed that the angel had opened a portal for healing right then and there. Through the eyes of his spirit he saw what he could describe only as "liquid glory light" flowing from an opening in heaven, filling a pool on the floor at the front of the church. When Pastor Denny Cline invited people to come forward for ministry, many who reached the area fell under the power of God before anyone had opportunity to lay hands on and pray for them. Several testified later that they had been healed of long-standing conditions, including back and neck injuries.

Meanwhile, the Lord continued his conversation with Todd. *Where have you seen this angel before?* God asked him.

Todd, no stranger to angelic visitations, nevertheless answered, "Lord, I've never seen this angel."

Then God brought to Todd's memory an intense season of

spiritual soaking in early 1998. During this three-month period Todd had spent several hours daily immersed in the Spirit and waiting on the Lord. *Do you remember the day you saw an angel towering through the ceiling of your apartment?* God asked.

"Yes, Lord."

That was this same angel, God told him. *This is* your *angel. It's because of this angel of revival that I've ministered through you in such power all over the world, as young as you are. Don't forget it.*

The Lord went on to explain how this angel had been involved in various historical revivals. Todd heard God say clearly, *Scotland.* Then he spoke a name Todd did not recognize: *John Knox.* Although Todd had never studied church history, he knew from this word that someone named John Knox in Scotland must have received this angel's ministry during a move of God's Spirit.

A week later Todd stood worshiping in a service at Portland's Shekinah Christian Ministries, where he would preach later that Sunday morning. Abruptly he found himself taken to Scotland in a trance. He had no familiarity with Scotland, but knew in his spirit where he was. He saw a large castle and the details of its architecture, including a surrounding moat. He noticed a crag and rolling hills to his right. As he walked a couple hundred yards down from the castle, he came to the gravesite memorial of John Knox.

When Todd's trance ended, his thoughts wrestled with what he had seen. *I don't even know if this John Knox is buried in Scotland,* he realized.

At lunch after church that day, Todd shared his vision with Pastor Les Moore, who listened with interest.

"Todd," said Pastor Les, "John Knox was a great reformer of the sixteenth century." He told Todd some of Knox's story, and confirmed, "John Knox is buried in Edinburgh, Scotland."

Now Todd knew the city where his trance had taken him. As he continued to ponder these revelations, he wondered what God was saying.

Within days, Todd received an e-mail note from Catherine Brown, a gifted prophet in Scotland, inviting him to speak and minister in that nation. Todd marveled as he read it. "OK, God, I get the message—I'll go!"

During April 2001 Todd toured five cities in Scotland, preaching and ministering as the Holy Spirit empowered him. The last city was Edinburgh. Todd shared with the pastor there about his experience with the angel and the trance.

The Scottish pastor not only confirmed everything but took Todd personally to the site of his vision. Just as he had experienced in his trance in Portland, Oregon, Todd visited the castle, saw the crag and rolling hills, and went to the nearby John Knox memorial. He felt exactly as though he had been there before—because, in the supernatural, he had.

The angel called Revival continues to minister with Todd. The Lord has told him he has a commission from this angel not just to release God's healing power on the sick but to impart healing anointing to the body of Christ for fruitful ministry, so whole cities will be touched and transformed.

Todd believes God is already opening the heavens and beginning to pour the rain of the Holy Spirit for healing and salvation. "Many places are going to receive such an outpouring of rain that pools of water are going to form like in John 5, the pool of Bethesda," he says. There God will minister in miracles, signs, and wonders that will bring the lost and hurting to find a Savior who loves them. Todd issues this challenge: "Will your church be a pool of Bethesda for the sick and the lame? Well, then let it pour, and the Lord says that truly they will come from miles around."

A Dream Reveals a Healing

In chapter 3 we met young Kari Morse, when she prayed for healing of her mother's burned hand. That sign followed another, even earlier, supernatural experience.

A nasty flu bug ravaged the Morse household during

December 1999. Dave and his wife, Kathi, each weathered a terrible bout. Even Kari, not quite four, and fifteen-month-old Aaron got hit.

While the others recovered over time, Kathi was never quite the same. Congestion eventually cleared in her chest, but moved into her throat and larynx. Her voice, already a low alto, became thick and gruff. It often cracked, since her pitch range had shrunk to almost a monotone. Frequent coughing and throat clearing did nothing to relieve the gravelly sound of her vocal cords. Worst of all, she could no longer sing to her children, a favorite bedtime ritual.

Kathi kept hoping for change, but months passed with no improvement. Kari, in particular, missed her mama's singing. At bedtime when she asked for a song, Kathi had to tell her repeatedly, "No, Honey, I can't sing tonight. Maybe in another week." By the following summer, however, resignation had set in. Kathi began telling her daughter, "You know, Honey, my voice just isn't what it used to be."

Kathi, too, missed singing, because of the spiritual connection it provided with her children. Kari first asked Jesus into her heart at age three, and already had a childlike faith that often took her parents' breath away.

The thought of permanent vocal damage made Kathi wonder if she should finally seek whatever medical help might be available. At the same time, she felt a nudge from the Lord: *Why not ask me first?*

During the past year Kathi had heard the Lord calling her to intercession. She had gotten involved with the prayer team at her home congregation, Trinity Church of the Nazarene in Lompoc, California, fifty miles northwest of Santa Barbara. She found it especially exciting to gather with intercessors from all kinds of churches as they prayed over the Central Coast.

Trinity Nazarene, a church of about 650 including children, offered a Wednesday evening service that Kathi and Dave usually attended. By September 6, 2000, Kathi had decided that if no one else came forward that night asking prayer from the team, she would have them intercede for her voice and throat.

When the service ended, the thirty or thirty-five attendees began to disperse while prayer team members made themselves available at the front. No one requested prayer right away, so Kathi mentioned casually to a friend on the team, "If nobody comes up, I have something." Debbie agreed to pray with her.

Just then, however, someone appeared, and a small group gathered to intercede for this person's need. When Kathi and the others finished, everyone turned to go.

In that instant, Debbie remembered. "Wait a minute, Kathi—didn't you say you had something to pray for?"

"Oh, yeah," Kathi replied. "It's not urgent, but I feel like the Lord wants me to ask." By then only eight or ten people remained in the worship center, one of them her husband. Dave, serving with the sound crew that night, was busy coiling microphone cords.

Debbie and their prayer team leader, Melissa, stood alongside Kathi and asked her how she wanted them to pray. Kathi shared about the problems with her throat and voice.

Melissa responded with a question of clarification. "So what you're asking is that we pray for healing, right?"

Kathi realized that she had scarcely formed the thought, let alone the words, in such a specific way. Yet despite negligible expectation, she looked at her team leader and replied, "Yes. I want God to heal me."

The three women held hands in a circle, and Melissa started to pray. Almost from the beginning, Kathi felt a warmth rise in her throat. Because she had grown up in a Pentecostal church, she actually discounted the sensation. *I'm supposed to feel warmth when people pray for healing,* she thought, *so I'm probably just imagining this.*

At that moment a movement started in her throat. She felt contractions similar to swallowing, and her Adam's apple bobbed up and down—but she was neither swallowing nor speaking. As the movement began to be uncomfortable, Kathi wondered momentarily if it had come in response to the doubt her thought had just expressed.

OK, this is definitely not in my head, she realized. *Something is going on here.* At one point Kathi also felt weak-kneed, as though the Holy Spirit's manifest presence had come upon her. When she concluded God was touching her with his healing power, she felt a shock of wonder. *This is really happening! This isn't normal, but it's exactly what we're asking for!*

Without even checking her voice, Kathi knew God had answered. When Melissa finished praying, Kathi suddenly realized intercession was no longer appropriate. She looked up and squeezed Debbie's hand to signal her to stop.

"We need to thank God," Kathi told her friends.

The two went back to prayer, thanking the Lord in advance for whatever he wanted to do. Kathi squeezed their hands again.

"No, I mean we need to *thank* him," she repeated.

They looked at her quizzically. Melissa asked, "You mean thank him now? It's happening now?"

Kathi affirmed what she was feeling. The women began to rejoice and praise God for his healing. Strangely enough, Kathi's voice did not sound much different yet, but the Lord had given her faith that the work was done.

On the way home she told her husband what had happened. Her throat felt somehow lighter and less congested, but she knew the real test would come when she tried singing for her children.

At the house she found that her sister April, baby-sitting Kari and Aaron, had already put them to bed, so as Kathi got herself ready to retire, she started singing in the bathroom. To her joy, the sounds and tones of her normal voice returned. Overwhelmed with gratitude, she praised God for his supernatural ministry.

On Thursday morning Kathi went to wake Kari, knowing she would be thrilled to hear how God had answered her prayers for her mom. Yet four-and-a-half-year-old Kari had already had a visitation.

"Honey, Jesus healed Mama—I can sing again!" Kathi began.

Kari smiled, looked up sleepily with her dark hazel eyes, and said, matter-of-factly, "I know."

Kathi, sure her daughter had not understood, made another attempt. "Honey, did you hear me? I can sing again. Jesus healed my voice."

"I know, Mom."

"How do you know?" asked Kathi, baffled. "This happened last night after you went to bed."

Kari sat up a little more and told her mother a story. "Well, during the night, somebody came into my room. I wasn't scared, but I looked at him and said, 'Who are you?' and he said, 'I am God.' Then he came over and touched me on my head. He told me, 'Your mom's voice was healed at church tonight.' I was like, 'Wow!'"

Kari went on, "He told me that you were praying and you felt something and it was your voice being healed. I was so happy. I said, 'Thanks for telling me!' and he said, 'You're welcome,' and then went straight up. I said bye to him."

Dumbfounded, Kathi managed to say, "So then you dreamed all this?"

"Yes," her daughter answered. "I saw him in my dreams. But I wasn't sure if I was dreaming or if I was awake. He touched me, and he put it into my mind so I would dream it." Kari described Jesus wearing a white robe with a blue scarf, clothing similar to that in a picture she remembered from her preschool Bible.

When Kathi told Dave this story, they both marveled at the anointing of God on their progeny. Once again Kathi began singing to her children nightly, and judged her voice better than ever.

Several times Kathi has asked God why he chose to heal her

voice, when the condition was not dire or life-threatening. All she can discern is that through this healing her faith to pray for others has increased, and this testimony to both Christians and non-Christians has encouraged them, helped build their faith, and given glory to God.

As Kari grows in her walk with the Lord, her mom and dad pray for guidance in mentoring her and their son, Aaron, who accepted Jesus as Savior in the summer of 2001, just shy of age three. Whenever Kathi sings, she has opportunity to praise God not only for her healing but also for the supernatural ways the Lord is speaking to Kari and many others of the next generation.

Divine Dreams and Visitations: A Family Affair

Fear gripped Thiem Korsal. Pain and shortness of breath had once again driven her to the Emergency Department with a partially collapsed right lung. This third episode was the worst. Doctors measured her lung capacity as down by at least 50 percent. Now they had to consider serious treatment options, which sounded to Thiem almost as scary as her condition.

For some time Thiem had suffered recurring pain on her right side. At first she lay blame on an unknown injury or pulled muscle. Eventually she learned that she had a rare form of spontaneous pneumothorax, a condition in which air accumulates in the chest cavity, pressing on the lung and preventing proper inflation. This disorder normally occurs in tall, thin, young men. However, in the form plaguing Thiem, the symptoms followed her menstrual cycle. Activated by her monthly hormones, endometrial cells that had migrated to her chest cavity formed small blisters on her right lung. Air leaking through holes caused by the blisters created a painful bubble in her chest that restricted breathing.

Thiem brooded over the many challenges she and her husband, Charles, had faced since their marriage and her move to the United States. The two had met in May 1988 in her hometown of Udon Thani, in northeast Thailand. Thiem did bookkeeping for Charles' cousin at a Catholic missions school in Nong Khai, about forty minutes north on the border of Laos. Charles, working in Japan at the time, had taken a trip home to Michigan and detoured to visit his cousin on the way back to Japan. Later he confessed that when he arrived at the airport and saw dark-eyed Thiem in her green dress standing next to his cousin, he knew instantly, *That's the girl I'm going to marry.*

Charles, a tall, brown-haired thirty-two-year-old, and Thiem, twenty-six, married in Nong Khai in January 1989, but it took six months to get government permission for her to join him at their new home in Lansing, Michigan. The challenges of an intercultural marriage, on top of moves to Dearborn and then Ann Arbor, only added to the stress of Charles working weekends at a second job. While his training in technology provided good employment, he planned to enroll at Cooley Law School in Lansing and get a law degree.

After a full-scale spiritual attack involving demonic manifestations and nightmares drove them to flee their Ann Arbor apartment, the couple recognized the need to come into spiritual unity. Charles went step by step with Thiem through a simple Bible tract, and that afternoon she gave her heart to Christ.

The two of them also gave their marriage to him. They found a new home at a townhouse in Ann Arbor, as well as a church home. Their daughter, Frances, was born in late 1992. As the years passed, Charles enrolled in law school, Thiem began attending Cleary College of Business, and they both got jobs in the Information Technology department at the University of Michigan.

But then Thiem developed sharp pains on her right side, with the eventual diagnosis of spontaneous pneumothorax. When her lung collapsed for the third time, the week before Thanksgiving in 1999, doctors at the University Medical Center decided her lung was not going to reinflate by itself. In a torturous procedure, they squeezed a hard plastic tube into an incision between her ribs to pump the excess air out of her chest cavity, giving her lung room to regain its normal capacity.

For several days Thiem lay in her hospital bed while the vacuum pump bubbled like an aquarium beside her. Before it finished removing the accumulated air, a pulmonary expert and a professor of surgery came to a conclusion.

"Once you've had pneumothorax this many times, to this degree, there's a 90 percent guarantee it will happen again," one of the doctors told Thiem and Charles. The specialists recommended a surgery called pleurodesis. This procedure uses chemicals to scar the inside of the chest cavity so the lung bonds to it like Velcro, preventing collapse. "If you go ahead with surgery now, we won't have to reinsert the chest tube later," they added.

One more painful procedure sounded better than two. The doctors also gave good odds the operation would solve the problem.

As Thiem prepared for surgery, Charles called their pastor and intercessors at church to cover her in prayer. In the operating room, just before the anesthesia knocked her out, Thiem saw a bright light and someone standing at the foot of her bed. The tall being had shoulder-length, wavy hair and wore a translucent light blue sash over a brilliant white robe. She heard a voice saying, "You're not alone"—and then she went under.

Afterward, Thiem felt as though someone had scorched the inside of her chest with a hot iron. During her ten weeks of recovery, Charles had to drop out of law school for a term. Yet the pleurodesis seemed to do the trick. Every now and then, at certain times of her hormonal cycle, Thiem would feel a characteristic pain and tell Charles, "If I hadn't had the surgery, my lung would have collapsed today."

In early 2001 the Korsals began making plans for Thiem's mother, Bua Kong-un, to come from Thailand for an extended visit. With Bua a staunch Buddhist, the couple sensed a spiritual confrontation building. Some frightening nightmares tormented Thiem. She also suffered an attack of chest pain.

Charles and Thiem asked their pastor and an elder to come pray for Thiem and their home before her mother arrived.

About that time Thiem had another dream—a prophetic one. She saw herself walking at night down a path by her village in Thailand. All the villagers came walking the other direction toward her. They said, "Don't go that way—there's a very scary demon ahead, and he's going to get you."

Among the crowd Thiem saw her family members. They gave her the same warning, but Thiem replied, "No, I'm going home."

Then her mother announced, "I'm going with you." She turned around and began to walk with Thiem, clutching her hand.

The two went on together, and as they approached a particular tree an evil spirit lunged at them. Bua grabbed her daughter's arm, but the young woman just pointed a finger at the demon. "In the name of Jesus, depart from us!" she commanded. "Get away!" Instantly it bowed to the ground, cowering.

"See, Mom," Thiem told her, "if you say the name of Jesus, this thing is afraid. If you called on Buddha, it might not listen to you." Her mother marveled at the power of this name.

The two continued walking and soon arrived at home, happy and at peace.

Thiem shared this dream with a friend from church, who responded, "Thiem, I think the Holy Spirit is saying your mom's going to get saved!"

The idea that her mother would turn from her ingrained Buddhist practices could not quite push past Thiem's doubts. Yet the church joined in prayer as she and Charles awaited Bua's arrival on May the twenty-eighth.

The Korsals and their church family welcomed Bua with the love of Jesus. She began attending with them, Thiem translating as needed. At first Bua continued to wear a big Buddha icon, rimmed in gold, that had hung on a chain around her neck ever since she had stepped off the plane. After a couple of weeks, however, Thiem noticed that her mom had taken off the necklace.

On Sunday, June 10, their church held a celebration of baptisms on the shore of Clear Lake, about twenty-five miles west of Ann Arbor. Eight-year-old Frances Korsal joined those professing their faith publicly, as her grandmother watched.

Bua attended another happy gathering on Saturday, June 16: Thiem's graduation from Cleary College of Business. Yet two days later everything changed.

After Thiem went to work on Monday morning, she began to gasp for air, her right side throbbing. In desperation she asked her boss to call an ambulance and her husband.

Charles rushed to meet his wife in Emergency at the University of Michigan Medical Center. X rays confirmed the awful news: Thiem's right lung had collapsed again. Her doctors shook their heads in consternation that the chest wall-scarring surgery had failed to hold her lung in place. They made Thiem wait eight hours for another set of X rays, because sometimes a pneumothorax will resolve itself. When the lung did not reinflate, however, Thiem faced the dreaded plastic tube once more, jammed between her ribs to evacuate the excess air in her chest cavity.

For almost a week the vacuum pumped out Thiem's chest, taking pressure off her collapsed lung. Bua could not stop crying when she visited and saw her daughter in such distress, surrounded by mystifying machines making strange sounds.

When Thiem's lung regained its capacity, her doctors discussed options. Some urged her to undergo another pleurodesis. Still-horrifying memories of the first operation compelled Thiem to refuse. The chest tube came out and the medical team sent Thiem home, knowing future treatment would be necessary.

Three weeks later, at her next menstrual cycle, it happened again. Charles was working that Saturday, July 14, when he got a call from his panicked wife at home and came to take Thiem back to the all-too-familiar Emergency Department. Bua cried again as she watched them leave.

Charles and Thiem spent all day and all night at the hospital. Thiem was terrified the doctors would no longer allow her to reject a second surgery. Yet as the hours passed her lung recovered function. By five o'clock Sunday morning, the Korsals returned home.

Thiem's mother greeted them the moment they stepped inside. "You are healed!" she told her daughter. "You are healed!" Thiem, already discouraged about her prognosis and too tired to process what her mom was saying, went to bed. That evening, however, she and Charles sat down with her and heard an amazing story.

Bua repeated her assertion: "You don't need the surgery. You are healed. He told me."

"Who told you?" Thiem asked.

"After you left for the hospital yesterday, I went upstairs and knelt down to pray. I said—"

Thiem interrupted. "Who did you pray to, Mom?"

"Well, Jesus, of course," came the reply. "I said, 'Jesus, show yourself to me. If you are real, heal my daughter. Bring her home. Don't let her have this surgery. If she comes home without surgery, I will believe in you and follow you all my life.' I told him that. Then last night Frances and I were sleeping downstairs in the living room. I dreamed that someone touched my leg and woke me up. I was awake when I heard him say, 'Your daughter is healed. She doesn't need the surgery. She's coming home.' That's how I know. He told me. You are healed!" Bua concluded, confidence shining from her face.

Thiem, on the other hand, listened to her mother with doubt and wonderment wrestling for control of her thoughts. Yet more surprises lay in store.

A bit later Charles went to help Frances get ready for bed. Soon, however, Frances bounded back downstairs and told a story of her own.

"Mom, I just remembered something that happened before

Grandma came," Frances said. "I told Daddy and he said to tell you, too. I was in bed praying one night and wanted to go to sleep. But something held my eyes open and wouldn't let me fall asleep. Whoever it was wanted to talk to me. It started saying something like, 'Your mother is going to the hospital, but don't worry about it; she's not going to need surgery.' The voice used these big doctor words I didn't understand, like 'She's going to have this pneumothorax....' But it told me you'd be OK. It really wanted me to know. And after that I could fall asleep."

Thiem knew her daughter had seen visions before. This story only confirmed her mother's experience. Faith began to arise that God was indeed touching her with his healing power. As friends from church phoned and came by, bringing food and flowers, the Korsals told them everything that had happened.

Two weeks later their pastor preached about salvation. At the altar call, an elder crossed the sanctuary to Thiem and Bua. With uncharacteristic boldness, he asked Thiem to translate this message: "Tell your mother I think God is saying, 'Today is your day!'"

Thiem asked her mom if she was ready to follow Jesus and accept him as Savior. She nodded. Despite Bua's usual reserve, she agreed to go forward for prayer. With Thiem translating, a few ministry team members led Bua in prayer to confess her sins and receive God's forgiveness and salvation through Christ. Thiem felt the overwhelming presence of the Holy Spirit as her mother wept and wept.

Charles and Thiem found someone who tracked down a Thai Bible for them. At first Bua's poor eyesight kept the pages out of focus, but then Charles needed to replace his reading glasses, and Thiem got an idea. "Charles, let me see if your old glasses will help Mom read the Bible."

They did. Soon Bua could not put the book down. She soaked up the words on its pages, reading it for four to eight hours a day, memorizing large sections at a time.

In August the Korsal family took a vacation. On their way north to Mackinac Island they stopped at Grand Haven, on Lake Michigan's eastern shore. Bua brought her Buddha necklace and asked Charles and Thiem to help peel off the twenty-four-karat gold into a plastic bag. Then she and her granddaughter took the icon to the end of the pier, where Frances flung it into the water. Thiem recalls how she told the story to friends when they returned: "We walked out on the pier that afternoon and said good-bye to Buddha. Now he's at the bottom of the lake!"

Although the devil challenged her faith, Thiem fought successfully for her healing. Once a month through that fall she felt her right side begin to hurt again. Each time she declared to the heavenly realms, "Devil, get away from my life. I am healed now." As she praised and thanked God for restoring her body, the pain left.

Thiem had another dream. She watched Charles and her brother fishing in a lake, with Charles catching one fish after another. At first Thiem fussed, because she wanted to land some too. Yet her husband gave her everything he caught, and that made her happy. Then she saw her brother pull the plug on the lake. The water drained out and they collected many more fish easily.

Charles and Thiem pray this dream, too, will prove prophetic. Bua tells them she wants her youngest son to become a pastor. The family has asked their church to intercede with them that another person in Bua's family and another person in her village will come to faith in Jesus, so she will not have to walk out her faith in isolation.

Job 33:14-18 describes how the Lord uses dreams to communicate, even with unbelievers: "For God does speak—now one way, now another—though man may not perceive it. In a dream, in a vision of the night, when deep sleep falls on men as they slumber in their beds, he may speak in their ears and terrify them with warnings, to turn man from wrongdoing and keep him from pride, to preserve his soul from the pit, his life from perishing by the sword." Since night visions seem to run in the family, perhaps God will choose such a sign to draw other loved ones of Thiem Korsal to recognize his power and saving grace through Jesus Christ.

FIVE

Creative Miracles and Unusual Healings

THE BOOK OF ACTS recounts an explosion of power ministries that took place after the outpouring of the Holy Spirit at Pentecost. Amid many signs and wonders accompanying the spread of the gospel message, the text describes this situation in Ephesus: "God did extraordinary miracles through Paul, so that even handkerchiefs and aprons that had touched him were taken to the sick, and their illnesses were cured and the evil spirits left them" (Acts 19:11-12).

If Luke, the writer of Acts, describes these signs as "extraordinary miracles," can we assume some other kinds rate as simply "ordinary miracles"? Whether or not any move of God's supernatural power could be considered ordinary, some certainly cause more wonder and marveling than others.

One category that might be called creative miracles involves restoration or creation of physical matter, whether body parts or other material objects. When Jesus healed the man with the shriveled hand in Mark 3:1-5, something visible happened to restore his flesh and bones on the spot. Luke 22:49-51 says that when Peter's sword slashed off the right ear of the high priest's servant in Gethsemane, Jesus "touched the man's ear and healed him." Scripture does not explain whether Jesus picked up the severed ear and miraculously reattached it or if a new external ear grew—in whole or in part—to replace the bloody wound. In any case a creative miracle occurred.

Stories like these are taking place today, in the United States. God, who established the laws of physics and the forces of nature, stands above his creation and in control of it. He may choose to operate through natural laws or to override them, as suits his purposes.

The apostle John closes his Gospel noting, perhaps with regret, that even unlimited space in countless books could not contain the full record of all Jesus did. This little book, too, does not have room to tell about the grandson of a Fuller Seminary professor, born without ears, who grew external ears as well as ear canals; the woman whose eight-pound canned ham fed eighty-six people in a homeless shelter, with slices left over; the young man in Las Vegas who gained three inches of height instantly; the numerous people all over the country who have seen dental fillings and gold crowns materialize in their mouths; and so many more folks with incredible stories of God's glory displayed through supernatural works of wonder. Heaven alone knows the extent of all that God is doing. Here are just a few snapshots.

Jesus Comes to the Doughnut Shop

An empty gas tank ensured that David Prater did not miss his divine appointment at the doughnut shop.

On Friday, June 8, 2001, David finished his early shift as a volunteer at the 11th Hour Television Ministry in Modesto, California, eighty miles east of San Francisco. In addition to running cameras, he helped coordinate intercession for the program. That very morning he and another volunteer had cried out to God for more opportunities for one-on-one ministry to people in need.

David and his wife, Sheryl, have extensive experience seeing the power of God poured out through prayer ministry. Both of them grew up and still live in Ripon, about ten miles northwest of Modesto. David worshiped at the First Congregational Church of Ripon as a child, drifted far from God, then encountered the Holy Spirit in May 1974 in a radical reconversion that saved his marriage. David and Sheryl, while attending the Congregational church once again, also began pastoring a fellowship in their home in the mid-1990s. Over the years the growing group has witnessed countless manifestations of divine power to heal and to save. David, in his early sixties, now serves full time with Wings of the Wind Ministries, while his wife works for the city of Ripon in the Planning Department.

As David left the 11th Hour television studio that Friday morning and climbed behind the wheel of his 1995 Nissan Maxima, he intended to buy gasoline closer to home. Yet when he saw the yellow dashboard light warning him the tank was dangerously low, he decided to put in a few bucks' worth of fuel right away.

Once he made the stop at the gas station, it was an easy choice to drop in at nearby Baker Boy Donuts, his favorite doughnut shop in Modesto.

When David walked into the store sometime after ten o'clock, he found his friend Rom Bun working the morning shift. Thirty-three-year-old Rom and her husband, Seng Bun, pastor a Cambodian congregation in Modesto called the Church of Paradise and do church-planting work in Cambodia. From time to time people come to the doughnut shop to ask for prayer, or Rom will offer to pray for people. This day was no exception.

Rom, sitting at a booth with another woman, greeted David and asked him, "Pastor David, would you pray for this lady?"

"Sure, I'd be happy to," he responded. Rom got him a cup of coffee and two doughnuts, and then he joined Rom and her friend Harriet.

David talked with Harriet about her ministry needs, which included neck and back pain. He also learned that the middle-aged woman was troubled spiritually, and he prayed with her to rededicate her life to Christ.

David then had Harriet stand so he could pray for the Lord to touch her spine. As he often did, he first asked her to hold her arms straight out in front with her wrists together. Although an admittedly unscientific measurement, this check sometimes suggests shoulders out of alignment or one arm shorter than the other. In Harriet's case, the bases of her wrists were about an inch apart. David prayed for them to even up, and they did.

He then laid a hand on the back of her spine and neck and prayed in Jesus' name for healing of the root causes of her pain. When he finished, he said to Harriet, "Now try doing something you couldn't do before."

Harriet bent over and touched her hands to the floor. She shrugged her shoulders all around. She raised her arms over her head and declared, "The pain is gone!"

"Thank you, Lord!" David exclaimed. "Jesus, would you bless her now?"

Harriet's eyes filled with tears. Her body began to jerk in gentle spasms. Then she collapsed, and David caught her before she hit the floor. He sat her down carefully to allow the Holy Spirit to continue ministering to her.

The Holy Spirit, in fact, had much more to do. When David turned around, he saw a crowd of at least a dozen people who had entered the store. Undoubtedly most of them had come with doughnuts in mind, or coffee, or a drink from the refrigerated case. Yet now it seemed everyone's focus was riveted on the manifestation of the presence and power of God.

A small commotion at the booth behind him drew David's attention to a couple of Latinos pointing to their buddy and pushing him forward. The big man, probably in his thirties, could not speak English, and a woman nearby offered to translate. When David asked if the man wanted prayer, he held out his right arm. It was not just several inches short but actually withered—muscles shriveled, skin red and knobby.

Despite David's past experience praying for scores of short arms, he had never seen anything like this. He felt his heartbeat quicken as a thought raced by, *O Lord, what are you doing now?*

From his pocket he dug out a small vial of oil he carried for healing prayer, in accordance with James 5:14 ("Is any one of you sick? He should call the elders of the church to pray over him and anoint him with oil in the name of the Lord"). David anointed the man's deformed limb, and asked him to extend both arms. "In the name of Jesus and by the power of God the

Holy Spirit," David prayed, "I command this arm to grow out now!" An unction of divine authority came over him as he spoke to the muscles and nerves and ligaments, ordering all parts of the man's body to be healed, in Jesus' name.

Before the eyes of all, the man's arm quickly came forth, growing and filling out, until it looked just like his other one.

The man began to yell. He waved his arm and took off running around the shop. Excited shouts in English and Spanish filled the air as witnesses gave glory to God.

Lord, what did you just do? David marveled.

Then from the back of the crowd a Cambodian woman, about fifty years old, shouldered her way forward. "I want to sing for Jesus!" she rasped in a sandpaper voice. "I want to sing for Jesus!"

David noticed a long scar on the woman's throat across her larynx. Since he found her difficult to understand, he did not ask about the history of her injury. He simply anointed her throat and prayed as before, "In the name of Jesus and by the power of God the Holy Spirit, I command a creative miracle of a new voice box now!"

Almost immediately the woman fell to the floor and began laughing joyfully. Feeling a prophetic inspiration, David knelt beside her and spoke the Lord's blessings into her life—not only a new singing voice, but restoration in her family and equipping for service in God's kingdom.

After David said "amen," he looked up at the crowd, still standing agape, and sensed a sharp prompting by the Spirit that it was time for him to leave. He said good-bye to Rom and slipped out, with the wonder of Jesus' love still lingering in the doughnut shop like the aroma of freshly baked crullers.

Although the Lord rarely leads David to follow up on people for whom he prays, Rom later told him about her friend with the scratchy voice. At a refugee camp in Thailand several years earlier, Neigt Oung had had surgery to remove a tumor from her throat. The operation had destroyed her fine singing skills, leaving her in frustration and despair.

After her experience at the doughnut shop, Neigt not only regained her voice but started singing with the choir at the Church of Paradise, Rom and Seng Bun's congregation. God gave her a ministry as a guest singer at other churches. Her husband came into a new relationship with the Lord, and all six of their children now walk with Christ, some of them making radical changes from former lifestyles.

In January 2002 Neigt visited David and Sheryl Prater's home fellowship in Ripon. She shared her story of God's healing power, with additional details: She testified that her throat used to have a bend, but was now straight. Rubbing her hand up and down over her larynx as she spoke, she pointed out the formerly crooked spot. Then, radiating her joy in the Lord, Neigt sang a praise song to give God all the glory.

David continues to seek the Lord for ripe ministry opportunities wherever they may be found. They come with special enjoyment when they are served up alongside the best doughnuts in town.

Supernatural Orthopedics

"Bye-bye, Lucile! Bye-bye, Bennie!"

"Good night! Thank you so much!"

After a pleasant evening, Lucile and Bennie Powell left the warmth of company and walked out to the country road in front of their niece's house near Ellenton, Georgia, about ten miles east of Moultrie. Lucile looked forward to a good night's sleep after their drive home to the little town of Norman Park, about ten miles north.

In the darkness Bennie fished in his pocket for the ignition key to the station wagon, parked at the side of the dirt road, and did not find it right away. Reaching into the unlocked vehicle, he turned on its headlights so he could take a better look at his key ring. Lucile stood with him in front of the car as he emptied his pockets.

Down the road the beams of an approaching Mack truck swept around a curve. Lucile paid little attention as the rumble of the big engine grew louder; the road allowed plenty of room for the truck to pass.

Yet the Mack's driver, she learned later, was drunk.

Without warning the cab plowed into the back of the station wagon. The crunch of crumpling sheet metal and the tinkle of breaking glass filled their ears just before the wagon lurched forward with such force that it knocked both Lucile and her husband to the ground.

Bennie picked himself up, not badly hurt, but in the glow of the station wagon's still-illuminated headlights, Lucile could see something seriously wrong with her right foot. Broken bones stuck through her skin near the ankle, and the entire foot was turned around to the right, with her toes pointed backward.

Lucile didn't notice any pain right away. Calmly she told Bennie, "I can't get up. My foot's broken."

The sound of the crash brought relatives running from their niece's house. They carried Lucile to one of their cars and rushed to the nearest emergency facilities at a hospital in Moultrie.

There medical personnel prepared Lucile for transfer to a bigger hospital equipped for surgery. Orderlies held her down while a doctor quickly twisted her foot forward so they could put it into a splint. Now a bolt of pain shot through her foot and up her leg.

Bennie followed in the relative's car when an ambulance took Lucile some forty miles northwest to Phoebe Putney Memorial Hospital in Albany. For the next twelve days he visited often, as surgeons operated on his wife's foot and encased her leg in a cast up to her hip.

By the time Lucile left the hospital, doctors had replaced her big, heavy cast with one that extended to her knee. She wore this cast for several weeks before she healed enough to start working again.

Lucile's accident at age thirty-seven left the normally sturdy African-American woman with lingering and latent health problems. Sixteen years after that Saturday night on December 16, 1972, her ankle got to bothering her badly enough that she made an appointment with an orthopedic doctor in Moultrie. His X rays showed a surprise: a metal screw holding her ankle-bones together.

"Doctor!" she exclaimed. "I never knew that screw was in there!"

Infection raged throughout the ankle area. By removing the screw and treating the infection, the doctor got Lucile back on her feet, after another extended recovery period. Yet more troubles awaited.

Over time Lucile began to notice growing pain in her right hip. She felt the bone in her hip socket, perhaps weakened by the accident, slowly sliding out of joint. Unwilling to face expensive major surgery, she resolved to live with a crooked hip.

By 1999, however, the pain had become agonizing. She loved going to church but could not sit still. Twisting and turning in her seat, she tried to find a position that would bring some relief, to no avail.

On Tuesday, January 4, 2000, Lucile had a date to go shopping in Moultrie with her cousin and neighbor, Jennie Powell. Jennie came over, and the two prepared to leave together. As Lucile stepped out her front door, her right hip burned with pain and her whole leg felt as though it were barely hanging on.

"I hate to do it, Jennie," she told her cousin, "but I've got to make an appointment to get this hip checked. The bone's come out of the socket, for sure. I can't afford another doctor bill, but it's hurting me so bad." Lucile grimaced. "I'll have to call the doctor tomorrow. I can't go on like this."

The next day Lucile was alone in the house, as usual, after Bennie went to work. Still reluctant to contact the doctor, she let the morning pass without making that phone call. About noon she used the bathroom and was just coming out of the doorway when her body froze, stiff as a statue. Her right foot hung in the air, an inch or so off the floor, and she could not put it down.

O Lord, what's happening? Lucile wondered, a surge of fear welling inside. Her suspended foot left her immobile for some five minutes as she fought off rising terror and confusion.

Then Lucile felt something like two large, powerful hands grip her ankle. A massaging sensation of heat rose slowly up her leg. When the warmth reached the top of her thigh, Lucile heard an audible click. It sounded just like a clutch pocketbook snapping shut.

Lucile stood motionless for another minute or two before her right foot began lowering to the floor. Still scared, and with no idea what was going on, she thought she might fall if she tried to move. After a couple more minutes, however, she found she could slide her right foot forward on the floor.

Thank God, I can move again! she thought. After a moment she slid her left foot, too. Then, gingerly, she picked up her feet and padded carefully into the living room.

Her head still spinning, Lucile sat in her favorite recliner chair and tried to make sense of this experience. All of a sudden she heard a voice.

"Your hip is not hurting."

She glanced sharply to her left. The voice had spoken so clearly that she half expected to see someone standing there. Yet she knew she was alone in the house.

"Your hip is not hurting," the voice came again.

With a shock she recognized it was true. Carefully she pressed her hand onto her hip socket and felt no pain at all. As a holy awe grew, she stood and pressed the area again, then sat back down. Still no pain.

A tidal wave of realization now engulfed her. *God has healed my hip!* Lucile leaped up and hollered aloud, "Thank you, Jesus! Thank you, Jesus!"

Her arms raised in praise, Lucile began to walk around her

four-bedroom house—from the living room to the kitchen, around through a bedroom, and back again. She made four or five circuits, weeping and shouting in gratitude to God.

That evening when her husband came home, Lucile spilled out the news, including the tangible and audible manifestations of God's presence. "Bennie, the Lord Jesus came and put my hip back in place!" She also told her cousin Jennie, and she, too, rejoiced at the power and goodness of God.

After years of pain and months of agony, Lucile's hip has not bothered her since that day. Now when others testify to healings by the Great Physician, Lucile Powell can give him glory for one of his many specialties: She praises the divine orthopedic surgeon who reset her dislocated hip.

Histrionics, Hysteria, or the Hand of God?

Inside Alice Hudson's minivan danced the lively voices of five young teenagers just released from school for the summer. Classes had closed after a half day that morning, so Alice's fifteen-year-old son and two friends, along with her thirteen-year-old daughter and a friend, headed across town to a public swimming pool for an afternoon of fun.

On Wednesday, June 6, 2001, the outdoor pool near their home in Greenwood Village, Colorado, had not yet opened for the season, so Alice took the kids to Utah Park's covered swimming pool in Aurora, another suburb of Denver.

As they scrambled out of the minivan, Alice called after them, "Have fun! Be ready for pick-up before closing time at five o'clock!"

She watched them scurry off, and smiled as she pulled away. Rearing children had filled the biggest part of her adult life. After giving birth to a daughter and a son, now grown, Alice and her husband, Dale, had adopted three more—a boy and two girls, including their youngest, thirteen-year-old Amber. In addition, over the course of some twenty years the couple, both fifty-one, had provided short- and long-term foster care for more than twenty other children of all ages.

Alice and Dale had welcomed Amber to the Hudson family just two years before, in May 1999. Adopted through Adams County, Amber had appeared on a television program featuring children whose circumstances presented special challenges to adoption. Because her biological parents had abused drugs and alcohol, Amber had become her parents' caretaker. Her strong personality as a survivor had made her precocious and opinionated.

That year's difficulties had mushroomed when the Hudsons' twenty-one-year-old daughter had developed cancer. Dusty, in a wheelchair with cerebral palsy, had moved out on her own in January. However, she had developed a large lump on her spine, and doctors had determined it was a fibroid sarcoma. Complications of surgery and infection had contributed to a total of seven operations that year. Yet God had proved faithful in saving Dusty's life and restoring her independence. By January 2000 she had moved back to her own apartment.

Since then Alice had turned her attention to nurturing Amber. The sturdy young girl had made some friends in the neighborhood and at her middle school, and through the influence of her foster mother prior to adoption, Amber had come into a personal relationship with Jesus.

After Alice dropped off the kids at Utah Park that sunny June afternoon, she asked her twenty-year-old son if he could fetch them before the pool's closing time. He had to go to work, however, so about half past four, Alice headed out again.

As she approached the pool building, her eyes widened to see a fire engine and ambulance parked in front. *O Lord, please don't let it be one of my children,* she prayed reflexively. Then, a bit ashamed, she quickly amended her prayer to ask God's protection over all the children.

Her dread turned to anguish as she walked in. Distraught kids ran over, crying, "It's Amber! It's Amber!"

When Alice first saw her youngest on the far side of the pool, strapped to a backboard with a cluster of paramedics hovering around, denial rose as a flash of annoyed impatience. In her thoughts she wanted to admonish her daughter: *Amber, cut the dramatics and get up! Stop wasting these people's time!*

Yet when she got near enough, Alice saw Amber's eyes full of fear as she lay pale and stiff. Grabbing her daughter's hand, Alice reassured her, "Amber, don't worry. I'm going to come to the hospital. I have to get the other kids home, but I'm coming."

Amid the chaos, Alice learned little about what had happened. One of the girls tried to explain, but details didn't get filled in until later. It seemed Amber had come down an inflatable plastic slide and stopped at the end, sitting up. Her friend behind her hadn't realized Amber was still on the slide, and her feet had smacked Amber in the back. Amber had flipped forward and hit the top of her head on the cement under about three feet of water.

One of the firefighters told Alice they had called the Flight for Life helicopter to take Amber to Swedish Medical Center in Englewood, on the south edge of Denver. Alice did not realize until later the serious implications of this news. The helicopter is used only in urgent circumstances. In addition, Swedish has staff connections with Craig Hospital in Denver, which specializes in treating spinal cord injuries.

When the chopper arrived, paramedics lifted the immobilized Amber aboard, but would not allow anyone else to ride with her. Alice tried to phone her husband at his dental practice, but could only leave a message with his assistant that something had happened to Amber at the pool. She gathered her fifteen-year-old son and the neighborhood friends into the minivan and hurried to drop them off. When she arrived home, she praised God to see her husband already there.

By the time Alice and Dale headed for the hospital, it was past 5:30 P.M. Traffic kept them on the road for nearly half an hour. Then they waited in the Emergency Department for some time before being ushered into the "family room," which seemed to serve as the place where doctors broke bad news to the patients' loved ones.

The Hudsons waited and prayed together. Yet as time passed, Alice's worry grew. "Something is wrong, Honey," she said to Dale. "Why aren't they letting us see her? Why isn't anyone talking to us?"

The clock was pressing toward 7:00 P.M. when Alice got up to find a restroom. Just then a young man coming down the hallway greeted them. "Say, I recognize you two from church!"

Rick Gobel happened to be serving his once-a-month stint as the hospital's volunteer chaplain. He told the Hudsons he had been paged to the Emergency Department, and would try to find out what was happening.

Rick soon learned that the Hudsons were the very family he had been called to counsel. Alice marveled at how God had provided someone they knew from their church to sit and pray with them that evening.

Finally a man in a white coat bustled into the room and introduced himself. Dr. William Pfeiffer, a trauma surgeon, said that X rays and CT scans had confirmed their fears: "Your daughter has a broken neck at C-5," he told the Hudsons. They learned Amber was now getting an MRI in preparation for surgery. The hospital had called in a team of neurosurgeons, Dr. Pfeiffer said, to determine how best to forestall swelling from the traumatized spinal cord, because swelling could damage nerves controlling Amber's heart and lungs. "When your daughter is out of the MRI, we'll come back and let you know," he assured them.

Shocked silence filled the room after the doctor left. Dale, as a doctor himself, explained that a fracture of C-5 referred to the fifth cervical vertebra in the spinal column. Damage to the spinal cord at that level could paralyze the body from the base of the neck down.

Rick led the Hudsons in prayer before Alice, trembling, rose to make some phone calls. "We've got to get this on the prayer chain," she said.

One of the few numbers Alice knew by heart belonged to their senior pastor and his wife, Louis and Ginger Angone. Dale and Alice had been friends with the Angones for almost twenty years, since Pastor Lou's time on staff at Cherry Hills Community Church. When Lou had planted the New Community Christian Church in 1996, the Hudsons had helped form part of the core group, and Dale became an elder. This Evangelical Presbyterian congregation of about 150 now meets on the campus of Denver Seminary.

When Ginger answered the phone, Alice sketched the information they had so far. Ginger promised to relay it to the intercessory team. In addition, the Hudsons and Angones' cell group was having a family picnic that night at a local park. A watermelon Alice had agreed to bring still sat in the back of her car. Ginger said she would carry the prayer request to that group as well.

Among other calls, Alice phoned her sister in Texas. When she explained that Amber had a broken neck and faced surgery, she began to weep as the gravity of her daughter's situation came into clearer focus. "I don't know how I'm going to be able to take care of two children in wheelchairs!" she cried. "God, give me strength to get through this!"

Before too long, Kim and Scott Schroeder arrived, the first of several friends from church. Kim served as New Community's director of healing and deliverance. She and Scott joined Rick and the Hudsons in fervent prayer.

To Alice it seemed like forever before any medical personnel returned to talk with them. Finally a neurosurgeon and his associate walked into the room and introduced themselves. Alice watched Dr. Martin O'Bryan, who circled and paced back and forth like a dog looking for a place to settle.

He made several false starts. "I don't know how to say this.... I've never seen anything.... We can't explain...." Finally he just blurted it out. "We did two MRIs on your daughter. The scans show no damage to the spinal cord." Dr. O'Bryan described how a whole team of spinal injury specialists from Craig Hospital had examined the original films from the X rays and

CT scans and compared them with the results of the MRIs. The first set showed the vertebra not only dislocated but chipped. The second set looked normal in every way.

The Hudsons and their friends cried out in joy and praise to God. "It's a miracle!" Alice proclaimed. With rising boldness, she started witnessing to the doctors. "God has given me a miracle, because he knew this was beyond what I could bear. See, I already have a child in a wheelchair. God answered our prayers. This is a miracle!"

The doctors gaped at her with blank looks and just mumbled in response. "Yeah, OK, lady—whatever. We'll take all the help we can get."

"When can we see her?" Alice demanded.

The neurosurgeon explained that feeling and movement from below Amber's shoulder level, which she had lost instantly when she had hit her head at the pool, had just begun to return. He arranged for them to find her room, where a happy reunion took place. The Emergency Department personnel, who had cut off Amber's swimsuit and draped her with a sheet, still had the teenager strapped to the backboard, but her color looked good and she could now wiggle some of her limbs. Kim Schroeder anointed her with oil and led additional prayers for Amber's complete restoration, praising the Lord for the miracle he had already performed. Before their tear-filled eyes Amber regained full movement and sensation.

As they prayed and rejoiced, Pastor Lou and Ginger came in and joined them. They expressed astonishment to hear that a miracle had occurred.

"You know, I just saw Amber about half an hour ago after first arriving at Emergency," Lou said. "She was lying completely stiff and motionless, with her hands curled up like little claws on her chest. The poor girl was in the room all alone and looked quite scared."

"What?" Alice exclaimed. "You saw her before we did? How did that happen?"

Lou answered, "I didn't realize you hadn't seen her yet! I just told the staff I was Amber's pastor. Ginger and I have been trying to catch up with you guys since then—this is a big place."

During her reunion with her parents, Amber's talkative tendency made its reappearance as well. "Mom, I'm so sorry they cut off my swimsuit! I just hated when they did that. And that MRI machine—it was so loud and noisy! It really bothered me. And hey—could you get me something to eat? I'm starved!"

The doctors had put Amber on intravenous doses of corticosteroids as a precaution against inflammation of her spinal cord, and wanted to keep her overnight for observation. So they moved her to a room in the Critical Care Unit, where Alice prepared to bunk down with her daughter.

Throughout that evening friends kept arriving. All expected to comfort Dale and Alice in their time of crisis and were thunderstruck to find a celebration instead. Alice enjoyed recounting the story to each of them.

Sometime before midnight everyone else finally went home, and mother and daughter aimed at getting some sleep. Amber had been left in a head brace, and she gave the nurses fits when she tried to wriggle out of it. In the morning, while Dale went to work, Alice met with the neurosurgeon again.

Dr. O'Bryan repeated how Amber's initial tests had shown the injury to her neck at C-5, with the likelihood she would face life as a quadriplegic. He told Alice that more than forty doctors, most of them specialists from Craig, had reviewed the films and could not adequately explain the change from the first set to the later ones. He described his own inclination toward a theory that temporary paralysis could arise as a hysterical reaction to trauma. "But this syndrome typically occurs among forty-year-old women," he admitted. "It would be unusual to see it in someone of your daughter's age."

Alice almost laughed out loud. *Why do scientists have to go to such ridiculous lengths to rule out every conceivable alterna-*

tive, she wondered, *when the evidence of God's supernatural power is staring them in the face?*

She heard one nurse in the Critical Care Unit try to suggest Amber might have moved during the initial scan, distorting the image to show a break when none existed. Yet Amber still lay paralyzed then, and the X rays' images clearly showed the injury.

Further tests, X rays, and MRIs run on Thursday all confirmed no damage to Amber's neck. Alice was thrilled when one of the paramedics who had rescued Amber expressed his own conviction that a miracle had occurred.

Dr. O'Bryan could see no reason to continue the steroids, and wanted to release Amber. Yet Dr. Pfeiffer, the trauma surgeon, preferred to keep her one more night for continued observation. They moved her from the Critical Care Unit to a room in the pediatric wing, and one of Alice's neighbors spent Thursday night with her so Alice could get some sleep at home. By about ten o'clock Friday morning, Amber was discharged.

For the next week Amber had to take a prescription of oral cortisone. She said her neck felt a bit sore and stiff—nothing serious. Her main complaint stemmed from the ache on top of her head where she had hit the cement.

The hospital warned Dale and Alice on the night of the accident that local newspapers would be calling, and got their permission to release information to the media. A reporter from Channel 7 television did some interviews and put together a short clip he called "Miracle, or Mistake?" Dale showed the complete file of X rays and scanner films he had obtained from the hospital.

Then during Amber's Back-to-School Night in September at Dove Christian Academy, the principal allowed her to give her testimony about what had happened during summer vacation. Afterward, another parent approached Alice with a story that blessed her tremendously.

"I was a fireman on call that day," he said. "When I got to the pool and realized how seriously injured your daughter was,

I felt compelled to phone my wife and ask her to pray. She then passed along the prayer request to others. I can tell you that within minutes of Amber's accident she was already receiving a lot of intercession."

Overwhelmed with gratitude, Alice Hudson cannot stop thanking God for his mercy in allowing this miracle in her life. She is humbled to realize many people just as desperate may pray for a miracle and not receive one. Yet she speculates that, more than God's favor to herself, this supernatural manifestation may indicate that the Lord has a special purpose or mission for Amber, one that requires full use of her body.

In any case, several eyewitnesses now have an amazing testimony, with medical documentation, of how God touched a teenage girl with his miraculous power in a way that left doctors scratching their heads.

And Amber got a new swimsuit.

Taught by God to Read
The atmosphere buzzed with expectation as the women gathered for their weekend retreat. Brazoria First Assembly of God in Brazoria, Texas, about fifty miles south of Houston, had invited Pastor Bill Ollendike from Bethany Cell Church Network in Baker, Louisiana, as guest speaker. The "Encounter" retreat, called "Breaking the Chains that Bind," was part of the church's leadership training program.

Barbara Buchanan mingled with the other women at the church that Friday evening, September 28, 2001, a week shy of her fifty-fifth birthday. Her eagerness about the weekend ahead lit up a friendly face that belied her age. When a woman handed her a booklet and other material to read and complete, however, she sighed with familiar frustration. Once again she would have to ask someone to help her. Barbara could not read.

Over the years the petite extrovert had taught herself to recognize a few simple words, as well as numerals. Yet reading for comprehension lay beyond her ability in most situations, and she had learned a number of tricks to get by.

A disrupted childhood had contributed to Barbara's reading disability. When she was only two months old, her parents divorced after her mother rejected her parenting responsibilities. Her father, working in Washington, D.C., sent Barbara and her brother to live with an aunt in Texas. At age six Barbara moved back to live with her dad, although she shuttled back and forth between Washington and Texas frequently.

The school system had passed Barbara through first and second grade, but by third grade her teachers expressed growing concern about her lack of progress and hyperactivity. Advised that his daughter seemed unable to learn, Barbara's father pulled her out of school. He enrolled her in a special education program, but it did not help much, and she stopped attending after a year or so.

Many years later, as an adult, Barbara hired a friend to tutor her for a while, but her reading ability still showed negligible improvement. In general, Barbara taught herself what she needed to know through other means. She learned to drive, for instance, and when she repeatedly failed the written test, the examiner quizzed her orally. She passed with a score of 98 percent and earned her license.

Barbara's illiteracy didn't interfere with her special sense of the presence of God. She recognized his voice at times speaking within her spirit, and she longed to know him better.

Barbara married Charles Buchanan, and in 2000 they moved to Brazoria, where Charles' sister lived. For several months she attended the Baptist church, but switched to the First Assembly of God church in early 2001. In that congregation of several hundred, pastored by Dale Frankum, Barbara entered a new and deeper relationship with Jesus, with a commitment to hear and obey him with her whole heart.

Outgoing and energetic, she became a church greeter, joined the worship choir, and grew increasingly hungry to learn more about God through the Bible. Although she realized it only in hindsight, the Lord had primed her for a divine rendezvous at the "Encounter" retreat weekend in late September.

"Darlene, would you help me read this booklet?" Barbara asked her friend. Darlene Tielke, like most everyone in the church, knew Barbara had trouble reading. She gladly went through the retreat material with her.

As the evening progressed, Barbara sensed God asking her to yield herself to him in new ways—to invite him and allow him to empower her with spiritual strength beyond human ability. *You've relied on other sources,* he seemed to say. *Now I want you to ask me for help. What do you need? Press in to me for it; cry out to me.*

Barbara mulled over this message when she went home that evening, and God's presence intensified. She knew what God wanted: not a halfhearted request for help but a cry from the center of her soul.

On Sunday, September 30, after the retreat ended, Barbara attended the evening service. During prayer for personal needs, she stood with several people holding hands in a circle when her spirit burst forth with a desperation she had never felt before. She cried aloud, "O Lord, please teach me how to read! I want to know you better. I want to know the Bible. I want to read your Word. Help me, Jesus!" As the others murmured their agreement in prayer, Barbara heard in her spirit a clear answer: *Yes.* She knew the Lord was going to answer her plea.

Two days later Barbara phoned her friend, Carol Carpenter. As they chatted about different Bible passages, Carol cited 2 Corinthians 5:17. Barbara, with a King James Bible in front of her, carefully scanned the book headings until she thought she recognized *Corinthians.* Then she followed the numbers to the chapter and verse.

Carol read the passage, then challenged Barbara: "OK, Barb, now you read it!"

O Lord, help! Barbara thought, her pulse quickening. Her eyes fixed on the first word, her mouth opened, and she began

to read: "Therefore if any man be in Christ, he is a new creature: old things are passed away; behold, all things are become
new."

Silence enveloped the phone line for a moment, until Barbara
cried, "Carol, I can read! The Lord is answering my prayer!"

"Barbara, you can read!" her friend echoed with joy. "Praise
the Lord!"

From that moment Barbara began reading everything—
Scripture, newspapers, cereal boxes—as though she had been
reading all her life. "Big words" sometimes gave her pause, but
after a moment of hesitation they usually came to her. She got
out a pair of reading glasses and bought a copy of *The Learning
Bible*, in the Contemporary English Version. She began writing
also, a previously almost nonexistent skill.

The next Sunday, October 7, Barbara met with Pastor Dale
and some women after church. Several had heard news of her
healing, and now she demonstrated by reading her Bible in their
presence, leaving them amazed and thrilled at the miracle God
had done. Later that month she stood up after an evening service, with many people still milling around, and read aloud. She
stepped into the aisle from the end of the pew and read selections from Genesis 1 and Psalm 23 as a public demonstration
for the glory of God.

After another service, Pastor Dale sat down with Barbara and
several others and put her on the spot. "Here, Barbara—read
this," he asked, handing her a Bible turned to an unfamiliar passage. She figured he wanted to make sure she had not simply
memorized the selections she had recited earlier. She gulped as
some "big words" stared off the page at her, but read the verses
with no problem.

Rejoicing at her supernatural healing, Pastor Dale wanted
more people to hear Barbara's story and exalt the God of wonders. On Tuesday evening, November 20, Brazoria First
Assembly of God joined other congregations for a citywide
Thanksgiving celebration held at the Baptist church. Just before

the service got underway, Pastor Dale asked Barbara to go to the microphone in front and read aloud as a testimony to the Lord's supernatural power.

When Methodist pastor Terry Teykl from Renewal Ministries visited the church to lead an "Acts 29 Prayer Encounter" on January 12, 2002, he asked Barbara to write a short testimony of her healing, which he included as a sidebar in his book *Praying Grace: Training for Personal Ministry.*

Barbara's gratitude to God has drawn her into an even closer relationship with him, spilling out in love for others as well. She prays all the time for people and situations around the world, especially for the Holy Spirit to empower those facing situations beyond their capabilities.

In addition, Barbara says the Lord is now working on her spelling skills. As she cries out to him for divine help, as before, she finds him instructing her how to spell.

"The Lord is my teacher," Barbara testifies. "School isn't the only place where you can learn. Blessed be his holy name!"

Miracles of New Growth

"Louie, you've been under a lot of stress. Why don't you take a week off?"

Louis Gomez gladly accepted his employer's recommendation, although he would have to use his own vacation time. His doctor told him he was a walking stroke. Louie's full-time job in computer systems support at Universal Studios, northwest of downtown Los Angeles, paid well but called for him to deal with difficult situations daily. In his time off, he threw his energies into managing the jewelry business he had started in his hometown of Whittier, east of his job site by a thirty-five-mile commute.

In the relentless race to get ahead, Louie had set God aside. Every once in a while he thought about him, but had no time or desire to pursue a relationship he knew would demand a cost. His tank was dry, his needle on empty.

Twenty-five years earlier, life had looked very different. Louie had come to know the Lord as a fifteen-year-old in 1974 at a Victory Outreach church near downtown Los Angeles. He began witnessing at school and on the streets, enrolled in LIFE Bible College, and became involved in ministry. Then, at age twenty-five, in apparent good health, Louie came down with an illness that put him into the hospital for almost four weeks.

Believing Louie had an autoimmune disease, doctors prescribed a corticosteroid called prednisone to suppress his hyperactive immune system. Yet Louie's condition only worsened. For months he suffered a fever almost daily and developed painful, swollen joints in different parts of his body. A rheumatologist finally concluded that Louie had adult Still's disease, an affliction usually found in children that attacks the joints in a manner similar to rheumatoid arthritis.

By Thanksgiving 1984, when he was hospitalized again, a bitter weariness had formed a crust around Louie's heart. Yet a radio broadcast that weekend by Jack Hayford, senior pastor of Church On The Way in Van Nuys, revived his faith for healing. Over the next year he began to wean himself from dependence on the prednisone. By the end of 1985 God had completed a progressive healing that fully restored Louie's body.

Soon, however, his pursuit of career, combined with a bad ministry experience, led Louie away from regular church attendance. In 1995 he and two partners started Covenant Diamonds as jewelry design manufacturers and diamond wholesalers. They had private clientele, offering both custom designs and standard Christian pieces. By 1997 they had opened a store in Whittier, and the business expanded.

That same year a friend connected Louie with Harvest Rock Church in Pasadena, about fifteen miles northwest of his home. The church ran a bookstore offering a variety of resources before and after each service. Louie arranged to bring a display case of Christian jewelry for the store to sell, producing new business for him and a small profit for the church. Because he needed to transport and secure the pieces, Louie ended up attending services at Harvest Rock, and enjoyed listening to senior pastor Ché Ahn.

Another change had come in 1995 when Louie married Sybil, an African-American friend of six years. Her daughter, Amber Smith, never knew her biological father, so Louie became a father figure. Amber's move from a mostly black neighborhood to Louie's home in a white and Hispanic area of Whittier presented her with special challenges. She faced some racism at her middle school. Yet her leadership character and resilience remained strong. In eighth grade her peers voted her student body president. At home, however, her parents dealt with typical teenage rebellion issues, particularly after she entered high school.

Then in early 1999 Louie's computer systems job at Universal Studios found him working day and night on technical issues related to Y2K, the so-called millennium bug that many expected to wreak havoc when the clock ticked over to the year 2000. After a business trip that nearly wiped him out, his supervisors suggested a week off in March, starting two weeks before Easter.

With no plans to go anywhere, Louie decided to work around the house and yard. One of his projects, trimming trees, got put off until the end of the week, but on Friday, March 26, he borrowed a friend's hand shears and clipped the backyard trees. Early Saturday he finished trimming the two trees in the front. Then he faced two yards full of branches, many up to five feet long, that had to be bundled or bagged for pickup by the city refuse collectors.

Louie needed to get to the jewelry store by 11:00 A.M. With his wife out running errands, he solicited Amber's help cleaning up loose branches. They lined a metal trash can with plastic lawn bags and began collecting yard waste. Yet progress remained slow until Louie made a suggestion.

"Amber, we've got to change our method here," he said.

"I'll hold out the branches so you can chop them in half to fit the container. Then I can stuff each bunch into the trash bags." Louie handed the shears to the sixteen-year-old, who eyed the long, sharp blades with a mischievous grin.

"Gee, I could do some real damage with these," she joked.

The two tackled the remaining debris, Louie holding and stuffing while Amber chopped. They came down to the last bundle or two in the front yard. Then, in the blink of an eye, Amber made a cut that missed the mark and sheared off the tip of Louie's right index finger.

Louie felt little or no immediate pain, and the initial blood flow didn't alarm him. Yet Amber panicked. Hearing her cries of horror, Louie feared she was about to hyperventilate or go into shock.

"Amber, calm down! Listen to me," Louie said. He had to think fast. A problem from yesterday complicated the crisis: A branch in the back yard had severed the telephone line when it came down, and the phone company was not scheduled to repair it until that afternoon.

Louie told the shaking girl, "Amber, just go into the house, get a towel, and get my car keys off the dresser next to my bed." When she returned, he wrapped the towel around his still-gloved hand and drove the two of them to the Emergency Department (E.D.) at Whittier Hospital.

Technicians hustled him in but had no spare cubicles, so Louie lay on a gurney in the hallway. When a doctor finally came and removed his glove, they saw a clean cut that had sliced off his finger just above the end knuckle.

"Where is the tip of your finger?" the doctor asked.

Louie thought perhaps it was still in the glove, since a piece of the material was left hanging, but the E.D. personnel looked through it fruitlessly. Louie concluded the tip must have fallen out in his yard.

The doctor wanted to see if it could be reattached, but Louie's home now had no working phone. He decided to call his friend Fred Cavazos at the jewelry store, only five minutes from his house.

"Brother Fred, I need your help!" Louie blurted. Quickly he explained the situation and asked Fred to look for the fingertip near a certain tree in his front yard.

A while later Louie's wife showed up at the Emergency Department with the finger and some ice in a freezer bag. Distraught, Sybil told him how she had come home just as Fred found the piece on the ground. When she heard the story, her heart had started pounding like a jackhammer, and she had rushed to the hospital.

The E.D. doctors determined that they could not risk the fingertip's reattachment because of the threat of infection spreading to the rest of the finger. By this time Louie's pain sensors had jolted to life. The medical team gave him a pain pill and a tetanus shot, and took some X rays. They rolled a ribbed rubber cover over the finger stub, immobilized it with a metal splint, and wrapped the whole hand in gauze. They told him they could not stitch the end closed, but that the clean cut should eventually heal on its own. Then they put his right arm into a sling that kept his hand vertical against his chest, and sent him home with instructions to contact his primary doctor first thing on Monday for referral to a hand specialist.

The primary doctor could not get Louie in to see the specialist until Wednesday. Dr. Anthony Britto, a plastic surgeon with extensive hand experience, told him that the end of his finger bone looked fine and that the skin on the stump should close and heal by itself. At that point they would address the need for physical therapy for any nerve damage. "I'll see you next week," he said. "Just change the gauze."

Sybil helped her husband wrap a fresh dressing daily. The blood flow, pumping like a hose in the Emergency Department, tapered off day by day. Often Amber watched in tears as her mom unbandaged Louie's finger. She seemed heartbroken with remorse, and Louie had to reassure her, "Look, I know it was an accident. Don't worry about it."

During the weekend, the Lord had begun dealing with Louie. Even in the E.D., as he lay on his gurney waiting for help, Louie had recalled a passage of Scripture that seemed to speak to him personally with the words of the Lord: *When are you going to crucify your flesh, Louie? When are you going to die to self?*

By Sunday morning Louie had begun praying with a passion he had not felt in years. On Monday he dug out an old devotional book someone had given him during his hospitalization in 1984. He heard God calling him to draw closer, to shut the door to the world and let the Holy Spirit fill him. In the midst of Louie's psychological adjustment to the idea of living with a deformed hand, God refreshed him and implanted a seed of hope for healing.

I healed you before and I could heal you again, the Lord seemed to say.

"Yes, Lord," Louie responded. "I know you are the same yesterday, today, and forever. But I don't know about your timing—when I get my resurrected body, I'll be whole, for sure."

Louie began praying for the Lord to touch Amber's heart. The next Sunday was Easter, and Louie could not wait to go to church. His family came with him to Harvest Rock, where Ché Ahn preached a salvation message. When the pastor opened the altar for ministry, Louie sensed the Spirit prod him, *Why don't you go up and get prayed for?*

Feeling embarrassed about the eye-catching sling that held his injured hand, Louie rather preferred to savor the blessing of the service and go home. Yet the urge to seek prayer became insistent. In fact, Louie had the impression he should make sure Pastor Ché himself ministered to him.

For about half an hour he waited with many others for prayer or blessing. Finally Ché came down the line to where Louie stood. He told the pastor about his accident. Then, more out of obedience to the urgent prompting in his spirit than from true expectation, he said to Ché, "I believe God wants to heal me, to grow this finger out. Would you pray for me?"

Ché paused a moment, looking slightly taken aback. Then he said, "Louie, I don't have time for my doubts this morning. If you believe God wants to grow your finger, as your pastor I will stand with you in agreement in that prayer." He touched Louie's hand and said a brief prayer of command in Jesus' name before moving on to the next person.

As each day passed, Sybil helped Louie change the dressing on his hand, and he examined his finger. Eventually they no longer needed to wrap it, as the wound healed. Sometime during the week after Easter, he dreamed about seeing a sliver of fingernail on the stump. In another week or so, the dream came true: He noticed a bit of nail starting to appear. Week by week Louie and his family watched the nail form, extending the length of his finger. By May he had a complete, new nail bed. The finger stopped growing just about an eighth of an inch short of its previous length.

Harvest Rock Church hosted a conference starting on Tuesday, May 11, with Jack Hayford as the first night's speaker. Louie planned to attend with his friend Fred Cavazos. As he prepared to leave, Amber unexpectedly asked if she could come too.

Pastor Jack preached on the gifts of the Holy Spirit. When he gave an altar call, he invited people to come receive a baptism or initial filling of the Spirit, not specifically for salvation. Yet Amber nudged her stepdad and asked him to go with her to the altar. She wanted to give her heart to the Lord.

Louie went home on a spiritual high. When he returned to the conference the next morning, he sought out Ché Ahn during the break. "Pastor, do you remember praying for my finger?" he asked. Louie explained the miracle of growth that had occurred, then shared how his daughter had been born again the night before.

Ché stood agape to see the healed finger, with its new fingernail, and hear about the newborn life in Christ that had resulted from this wonder. Due to speak next, he asked Louie if he would share this testimony from the platform.

Louie bought Amber a Bible, and she became involved with the youth group at Harvest Rock Church for a time. After her high school graduation, she began attending a community college. Her boyfriend told Louie, "You know, she's always praying."

Louie continues to intercede for her as his number-one prayer assignment. He believes that the Lord took him through this experience for her sake, and that God has an awesome purpose for Amber's life.

When Louie returned to Dr. Britto, the hand specialist showed considerable interest in his finger and new fingernail, but maintained his scientific point of view.

"You told me it would be just a stump the rest of my life," Louie reminded him.

"Well, maybe there were some cells that got regenerated, some tissue that wasn't damaged...." Louie could hear Dr. Britto searching for a biological explanation. The physician kind of chuckled when Louie explained how his pastor had prayed for it.

Louie believes the Bible promises miracles as a natural outflow of the message of the gospel, because the gospel itself is the story of death, burial, and miraculous resurrection from the dead. He cites Romans 1:16, which says the Good News "is the power of God for the salvation of everyone who believes," and the apostle Paul's testimony in Romans 15:18-19 that he preached the gospel "by the power of signs and miracles, through the power of the Spirit."

Now whenever Louie looks at his right index finger and the knuckle where it was cut, the miraculous new nail bed speaks to him of God's power, while the finger's slightly short length reminds him he is incomplete without the Lord. As we live out our destiny in dependence on Jesus Christ, Louie believes, he will demonstrate his authority over every area of the material and immaterial realms. For Almighty God, growing a new finger is no more difficult—and no more miraculous—than growing a new spiritual life from a once-dead soul.

SIX

Victory Over Darkness

NOT ALL GOD'S SIGNS and wonders bring direct blessing and benefit to his creation, although good in some form will always result. Sometimes he displays his supernatural power by bringing judgment on sin or evil.

In the Book of Acts, the instant deaths of Ananias and Sapphira (5:1-11) and Herod (12:20-23), as well as the sudden temporary blindness of Elymas (13:6-12), were signs pointing to God's omnipotence and holiness. The Lord, of course, prefers people to repent and turn from wickedness, as Ezekiel 33:11 and 2 Peter 3:9 make clear. Even when God prepares to exercise judgment corporately, he extends his offer of mercy as long as possible. The demise of Sodom and Gomorrah in Genesis 18:16–19:29 illustrates this truth. If only ten people had repented, even at the last moment, God would have stayed his hand. Instead, both cities and the surrounding area went up in smoke one morning as the Almighty rained down burning sulfur.

At times the Lord demonstrates his supreme power in acts directed against symbols of evil, rather than evildoers themselves. The rather amusing story in 1 Samuel 5:1-5 tells what happened when the Philistines captured the ark of the covenant, the resting place of God's Spirit, and set it in the temple of their god, Dagon. In the morning, "there was Dagon, fallen on his face on the ground before the ark of the Lord! They took Dagon and put him back in his place" (v. 3). Yet the next morning, their idol had not only fallen again but broken into pieces.

The Lord also wages war against the kingdom of darkness by liberating its captives, robbing the enemy of his spoils. This deliverance commonly takes place individual by individual.

Sometimes, however, spiritual warfare over an extended family or community will lift a collective veil of deception keeping people in bondage. Then the entire group, now freed to see and understand the truth, may cast off its shackles, repent of sin, and turn to faith in the Messiah. The "before and after" changes in such cases are often nothing short of miraculous.

Like it or not, we must acknowledge that the kingdom of God and the kingdom of Satan are locked in combat for human souls. First John 3:8 describes this warfare as the purpose of Jesus' coming to earth: "The reason the Son of God appeared was to destroy the devil's work." Ignorance of the cosmic battle only makes us more vulnerable to the enemy's schemes (see 2 Cor 2:11), because the devil operates in supernatural power just as God and his angels do. Yet as we put on our spiritual armor (see Eph 6:10-18), seek discernment and divine guidance, and live in holiness, humility, and dependence on God, we have assurance that the Lord will bring victory over the darkness.

"The weapons we fight with are not the weapons of the world. On the contrary, they have divine power to demolish strongholds" (2 Cor 10:4). If this is true of the arms with which the Lord has equipped us, imagine the power God can wield with whatever spiritual arsenal he may have reserved for his exclusive use.

Confronting Demonic Footholds in the Arts

Pulling into the driveway of his Colorado Springs home, Thomas Blackshear II said another prayer of thanks for God's provision. His spacious home was not only his residence but also his place of work. A nationally acclaimed artist, Thomas had set up a basement studio where he could work on his collectible sculptures, plates, prints, and other designs. In particular, his award-winning *Ebony Visions* line of figurines, reflecting his visual conceptions as an African-American, gave him special joy to create. *Lord, you've been good to me,* he prayed silently. *All glory to you.*

On this Monday in May 1998, Thomas entered the house after his errand and found his wife, Ami, sitting in a living room chair, holding their three-month-old son. Elisha represented God's special blessing to them, since Ami had suffered several miscarriages in the years before his birth. Yet today Thomas did not see contentment on Ami's face as she held their boy, his curly brown locks pressed against her chest. In fact, Thomas did not know how to read her expression.

"What's the matter, Ami?" he asked. "Why do you look like that?"

Ami fixed her eyes on her husband. "Thomas, you've got to clean out your studio."

He knew right away she was not talking about dust and clutter. He sat down and listened intently as she told him what had happened that afternoon.

Ami had needed to use the copier in the basement, and had brought Elisha downstairs with her—the first time the baby had been in his father's studio. There Thomas kept his art reference books, many collected during his fourteen years as an illustrator. The books showcased the work of artists Thomas admired for their keen talent, even though some of their subject matter included themes from science fiction, fantasy, sword and sorcery, wizardry, and similar genres.

Ami had set the baby down and gone to make the photocopy. Suddenly Elisha began screaming and flailing his arms, as though trying to brush something off of himself. Alarmed and baffled, Ami picked him up, but he remained inconsolable. She hurried back upstairs with him, and as soon as she got to the top step, Elisha became as calm as a lullaby.

Ami's mind reeled. *Well, I wonder what that was all about?* She felt troubled, but still needed to make her photocopy. So she returned downstairs with Elisha to finish what she had been doing.

Again the baby started to cry and thrash. This time, however, Ami herself saw something—a dark form that rose in front of her. Although seized with fear, she felt a presence within her urge, *No, stand and fight!*

Ami rebuked the evil spirit and claimed the power of the blood of Jesus Christ. Soon the figure disappeared—and in that moment, Ami recalled to her husband, their distressed baby had fallen into a serene sleep.

"Thomas, you've got to clean out your studio," Ami repeated, still shaken at the memory.

He didn't want to hear it. His precious book collection represented years of studying and acquiring the work of his favorite artists and mentors. Yet after listening to Ami's tale, he acknowledged that she was right. If any demons lurking in his studio were going to have that kind of effect on his son, he knew he had to take action.

Thomas called his friend Janie McGee and asked if she would come pray through his studio with him. With her gift of discernment, Janie could help identify items that needed to go.

The next morning, before coming to the Blackshear home, Janie phoned Thomas. "You know, as I prayed about this, God told me the name of this thing you're dealing with," she said. "It's a spirit that attaches itself to artists, or the arts."

Moreover, when Janie arrived that afternoon, she had had another revelation. "When I was driving over here, God showed me what this thing looks like," she told Thomas. "What I saw looked like a lizard, with a long neck and a long tail, big bat wings, and two clawed feet."

Thomas muttered, "Well, that's interesting," and took Janie to the studio.

For the rest of the afternoon they sorted through Thomas' shelves, praying and picking out items that could provide entrance for demonic spirits. All of a sudden, Janie looked up and cried, "Thomas! That's it! That's the thing I saw!"

Thomas turned to see his friend pointing to one of his favorite sculptures, hanging from the wall and positioned as though flying. It was a gargoyle. He had created the piece years before as a sample of his talent at a time when he had hoped to get work with Lucasfilm in special effects.

"Oh, man, don't tell me that!" Thomas groaned. He considered the sculpture one of his best. "You mean I'm going to have to take this thing and destroy it, right?"

"Well, I would," Janie replied.

With reluctance but resignation, Thomas pulled down the gargoyle and began to break it up. Made of Sculpey, a brand of plastic-based clay that can be baked hard, the creature had wings and tail each about a foot and a half long. When he had finished the demolition, he put the pieces into a bag, gathered the books he and Janie had culled from his shelves, and took everything out to the garage until the garbage collectors came.

Thomas knew he had more cleaning to do, but the major items were now gone. Everything seemed fine—until two days later.

On Thursday Thomas was on the phone in the kitchen when he heard a tremendous crash from directly upstairs in the master bathroom. He yelled to his wife, "Ami, what was that? What did you drop?"

Hearing no answer, he called again, with no response.

Just then Ami picked up the extension phone upstairs and spoke, her voice unusually insistent. "Thomas, you need to come up here."

Thomas told his friend he would call back, and hurried to the master bedroom. There stood Ami, her face pale, holding Elisha close. She told her husband she had been tending to Elisha in his bassinet, set between their bed and the doorway to Ami's side of the double master bath. In the background of her field of view she saw a big bottle of soap powder being lifted from a shelf on the far wall of the bathroom by an invisible hand. The bottle flew through the air toward the baby, but then suddenly dropped and shattered on the bathroom floor.

Ami and Thomas sensed that a demon stirred up from the basement cleaning was lashing back in anger. Thomas felt especially nervous because he faced an unavoidable weekend business trip, leaving Ami and Elisha home alone for two days.

Each night Thomas phoned from his hotel room to see how things were going and to pray with Ami. She told him she kept hearing noises from the basement, although nothing seemed to come upstairs.

When Thomas returned home late Sunday night and learned that the manifestations had not stopped, he decided to go from room to room, anointing the house with oil, before he went to bed. Nervous but determined, he forged ahead.

After he anointed the den, Thomas switched off the lamps on a side table, which displayed many framed family photographs. He had just turned to cross the room and flip the switch for the main overhead light when he heard a horrific clatter behind him, as though every picture had been knocked flat. Instantly he swiveled around, but what he saw gave him chills. Nothing on the table had moved.

This blatant manifestation stirred the Spirit of God in Thomas. He began to rebuke the demon boldly in the name of Jesus. With new strength, he finished anointing every room in the house. He even went down to the basement, hairs standing on the back of his neck, to speak the Word of God against the evil spirits. When he finished what he needed to do, he went to bed.

A week later Thomas and Ami finally managed to arrange a visit by a pastor from their congregation, New Life Church. Joseph Thompson, a Nigerian-American, prayed through the house with them. Afterward, no more manifestations plagued the Blackshear home.

During that week, the Lord gave Thomas an eye-opening revelation about the roots of this demonic oppression. He took Thomas back in his memory to age six, when his family had lived in Plattsburg, New York, near the Canadian border. His parents had returned from a trip bringing presents: a doll for his sister and a comic book for Thomas. Splashed across the comic book cover was a gigantic, flying gargoyle.

Young Thomas had never seen such a creature before. He could hardly take his eyes off of it. The pictures mesmerized him. In this way, God revealed, an evil spirit had found entrance and had begun to attach itself to Thomas' soul.

Thomas recalled how the monster motif had grown with him. Throughout elementary school and beyond, he had drawn gargoyles constantly. In high school he had first tried to sculpt one. Later the creature had popped up in his art school assignments again and again, like a mascot.

He realized his attraction to fantasy movies had sprouted from the same source. As the extent of its hold on his life grew clear, Thomas became agitated.

"Lord, how could you let this happen?" he prayed. "I was just a little kid. How could I have known the danger involved?" Thomas cried out, "Lord, I'm forty-three years old. From the age of six I have never lived without this thing's influence. I feel like I don't even know who I am without it!"

Into his troubled heart the Lord began to speak. *Thomas, I've always been with you.* God called to Thomas' mind his three primary Christian paintings: "Forgiven," "Watchers in the Night," and "Coat of Many Colors, Lord of All." *Remember, you did those paintings with that evil spirit still attached.*

Thomas realized that, despite the demonic oppression, the Holy Spirit must have held the upper hand all those years. Only by the Spirit's empowerment could Thomas' paintings have touched so many thousands of lives and prompted countless miracle testimonies. The compelling image in "Forgiven," perhaps his most famous work, shows the risen Jesus tenderly holding in his nail-scarred hands the slumped figure of a man still grasping a sledgehammer and a spike.

That night, Thomas sat in bed while Ami held their baby in the rocking chair. He told her everything that God had revealed. Emotion overwhelmed him, and he started to weep.

Ami, after listening quietly, responded, "Thomas, I think God is telling me to tell you something now."

"Well, what's that?"

"I believe he's asking me to tell you, 'Get rid of your comic books.'"

Thomas groaned. Collecting comic books, as well as art books, was one of the few relaxing hobbies he enjoyed. He protested, "But why? I'm not into them in a bad way! All I do most days is sit here working in these four walls, and just for a little pleasure I might go to a bookstore every once in a while. What's so wrong with that?"

"I'm not saying anything is wrong with that," Ami replied. "I'm just passing along what God's telling me to tell you."

"But this is too much!" Thomas cried. "He's taking away all this stuff at once, things that have been part of my life forever. Do you understand what I'm going through?" He looked straight at his wife. *"I'm dying.* When most people go through a spiritual death, it's a gradual process. But God's doing this all at once. And it isn't easy!"

Ami expressed empathy for her husband's torment. Still, she repeated the message. "I really feel God is saying that if you're obedient, you'll be blessed, and you'll see him work in your life like never before."

Thomas knew the Lord was speaking through his wife, but he could not deal with it just then. After a couple of days, however, he yielded his will. He gathered his comic books into six large bags and took them to a commercial shredding company.

After all this, Thomas reflected on his son's role in these events. During the first month of Ami's pregnancy, God had told her she would have a boy, that his name should be Elisha Thomas, and that he would have the gifting of a prophet to speak the proclamations of God to others, including people from developing countries. Thomas had responded to this message a bit doubtfully until the Lord had confirmed it to him the very next day.

Now, at just three months old, Elisha had shown his sensitivity in the spiritual realm by discerning and reacting to the presence of evil that had remained outside of his parents' aware-ness. Through the anointing on his life, Elisha had alerted them to the demonic danger in their home.

Moreover, when Thomas asked God why he had waited so many years to reveal this evil spirit's hold upon him, he heard God answer, *You wouldn't have listened to me before. I had to use your son to get your attention, because I knew you would do what it took to make sure he did not grow up with that influence.*

God had still more work to do in Thomas. Later in 1998 the Lord brought him into a season when he pulled Thomas back from all his painting. Although the artist continued work on his collectible figurines, he sensed God telling him to shelve his painting projects. God's hard message: *Rest in me. Reflect. Seek my face. This season is going to be very painful, but it's necessary to bring you into the purpose I have planned for you.*

For more than two years Thomas endured the process of refining. During this period he and Ami also underwent major renovation of their home and studio, and the Lord showed him an allegory: *Right now you see your home all torn up and a mess, but one day it will be very beautiful and functional. The same thing is happening to you spiritually now. After this difficult but needed season, I'm going to bring forth something beautiful in you.*

Divine messages came from intercessors, too. Three or four people independently told Thomas they sensed God giving him a prophetic anointing on his work.

When God began bringing Thomas out of this period, his excitement bloomed as he realized that for the first time in his life he would now be painting without a demonic spirit attached. Everything seemed brand new, and he could hardly wait to see what God would do.

The first indication came after Thomas became inspired to paint an image of the Statue of Liberty. He contracted with DaySpring Cards to deliver the work, but a bad case of "artist's block" held him back from completing it. He missed his dead-line by months, to his utter chagrin. Then two different women, within a week or two of each other, phoned Thomas to say, "That Statue of Liberty image—I believe the Lord is asking me to tell you, 'You need to get that painting done now.'"

With that encouragement, Thomas found himself able to finish the work. Four months later, terrorist attacks on New York City and the East Coast changed the atmosphere of the nation. The delayed "Liberty" prints landed in Christian bookstores right around the week of September 11, 2001. They quickly sold out.

As Thomas watched the mind-boggling scenes on the television news that day, he could hardly comprehend how God had both inspired and timed his art for the events the Lord knew were coming. Thomas realized that he had created his first prophetic painting.

Thomas has come to see that God's calling on his life requires a deeper and more difficult level of obedience than that which most believers experience, and his son may have a double anointing. Maintaining spiritual sensitivity will play a key role in walking out God's purposes in each of their lives.

Many Christians whom Thomas meets either do not believe in spiritual warfare or do not know how to handle it. He loves to tell his story to help open their eyes to reality. "Do you believe in the Word of God or don't you?" he wants to say to skeptics. "Because the truth is, what it says happened in the Word of God still happens today."

Warnings From the Audible Voice of God

Easter Sunday morning, April 4, 1999: In the pre-dawn darkness James Goll and his family lay asleep at their home in Antioch, Tennessee, about ten miles southeast of downtown Nashville. As founder of Ministry to the Nations and a gifted prophetic intercessor, forty-six-year-old Jim was familiar with close encounters of the supernatural kind. Yet he had no reason to expect the audible voice of God that woke him from sleep that morning.

"In eighteen months 'the hunters' will begin to be released."

The words, clear and piercing, jolted him instantly to attention. While Jim had heard God speak to his external ears before, this time the voice came with an electrifying tone. His wife, Michal Ann, slumbered on beside him, but Jim felt a tangible divine presence permeate the bedroom, bringing awesome fear of the Lord.

In that charged atmosphere, Jim lay motionless as the Holy Spirit then began speaking internally with more revelation. Jim knew what the Lord meant by "the hunters." For many years Jim has had special concern for the welfare of the Jewish people, knowing that the welfare of the global church is tied together with theirs. One scriptural revelation of God's prophetic purposes for the Jews comes from Jeremiah 16:14-16:

"However, the days are coming," declares the Lord, "when men will no longer say, 'As surely as the Lord lives, who brought the Israelites up out of Egypt,' but they will say, 'As surely as the Lord lives, who brought the Israelites up out of the land of the north and out of all the countries where he had banished them.' For I will restore them to the land I gave their forefathers.

"But now I will send for many fishermen," declares the Lord, "and they will catch them. After that I will send for many hunters, and they will hunt them down on every mountain and hill and from the crevices of the rocks."

Fishers, as Jim explains in his book *Exodus Cry,* attract the objects of their interest with enticing bait to draw them to a desired place. Hunters, on the other hand, chase down their prey, pursuing them with intent to destroy. Through Jeremiah, God says he will use both benevolent fishers and malevolent hunters to bring Jewish people into the place of their destiny in him.

Now on Easter Sunday morning the Lord had revealed the specific timing of a new wave of persecution coming against the

Jews. As Jim listened to the Holy Spirit speak to his heart, he understood that hunters from the biblical "land of the north" would be released, besieging Russian Jews in particular.

The Spirit's inner voice continued: *As a prophetic act, your family will walk out a parable. You will move from your place of residence to another area that is secluded. When the time comes, you will be thrust forth quickly.*

Immediately Jim realized the significance of this act. The Goll home lay in a subdivision of Antioch called Hunter's Run. By moving quickly from Hunter's Run, his own family would demonstrate prophetically how "hunters" on the run, both human and demonic, would drive the Jews to seek a place of refuge and seclusion. The move would symbolically call God's people to run to him as their hiding place.

Jim remembered the occasions in the book of Jeremiah when God asked the prophet to perform a dramatic illustration of his message and purposes for the people of Israel. Among other acts, Jeremiah buried a linen belt (Jer 13), broke a clay jar (Jer 19), wore a yoke around his neck (Jer 27), bought a field (Jer 32), and offered wine to teetotalers (Jer 35). God still uses these kinds of object lessons today, Jim knew.

The Holy Spirit closed by saying, *There is a confirmation of this and a significant surprise awaiting you on your computer, on e-mail.*

As the first hint of daybreak began coloring the sky, Jim climbed out of bed and padded upstairs to his office. Going on-line, he picked up his e-mail and found a message from friends in Austria. Helmuth and Uli Eiwen pastor a church in Wiener Neustadt and have made sacrificial efforts to find and repent to Jewish Holocaust survivors from their city. They told Jim they felt a leading from the Lord to join him at a conference in Sunderland, England, where he planned to minister in six weeks. They also said they knew God was going to be revealing something to Jim about the Lord's heart for the Jewish people.

Jim read and reread the message. Finally he went back to the master bedroom and roused his wife. "Ann, the audible voice of God woke me up this morning."

Michal Ann, no stranger to hearing the Lord speak, expressed awe and wonder as Jim spilled the story. They both tucked away this news and waited to see what God would do.

Six weeks later the entire family, including four children aged nine to fifteen, flew with a team of intercessors to Sunderland for the "Revival Now!" spring conference hosted by Ken and Lois Gott. Jim learned that Sunderland's "quad cities" region, in northeast England on the North Sea, includes one of the largest Orthodox Jewish communities in Europe.

At the conference Helmuth and Uli received confirmation of their role in giving refuge to the Jewish people. What amazed Jim, however, was a prophetic word that came through Cindy Jacobs, founder of Generals of Intercession and another of the conference speakers. As Cindy prayed for Lois Gott, she declared by supernatural revelation that Lois had Jewish heritage, a fact Lois herself had learned only eighteen months earlier. Cindy then began to prophesy about an exodus of Russian Jews traversing the North Sea in search of safe haven. The time frame in Cindy's word matched the one God had spoken about in Jim's bedroom.

When the Goll family returned to the Nashville area, the issue of moving to a new house rose front and center. The children's school had recently relocated south, adding at least twenty minutes to their commute, so a change of residence would benefit them.

The Golls began looking at homes for sale. Eventually they came across property in Franklin, about twenty miles south of Nashville. The realty agent's sign hung by the road, but they could not see the house from there. Feeling an inner nudge, Jim decided to drive up the easement and take a look. As soon as the house came into view, Jim and Michal Ann turned to each other with eager glances. "This is the place!" Jim exclaimed.

They learned that the land included almost twenty-five acres of beautiful rolling hills. The asking price, higher than they could afford, did not deter their faith that God wanted the property for them and Ministry to the Nations. Michal Ann, in particular, did not waver even when the sellers took the property off the market in November. "This is our inheritance," she affirmed. "God will provide somehow."

Weeks later Jim stumbled across a gift he had received some years before and forgotten about: a pair of railroad spikes, spray-painted gold. When his family had lived in Kansas City, Missouri, Bonnie Chavda, a gifted prophet, had declared that the Lord wanted to "nail some things down," and would use Jim and Michal Ann like the railroad tracks that joined the east and the west of the United States, facilitating transport of people and cargo. Later, as a symbol of this prophetic word, Jim's sister, Barbara, had presented them with the two spikes, reminiscent of the historic gold spike that furnished the final link in the transcontinental railway.

Now as he gazed at the spikes again for the first time in years, Jim knew what God had purposed for them. Although the acreage in Franklin was no longer for sale, he and his family and a ministry assistant decided to do a prophetic act over the land. After driving up the easement from the road, Jim parked the van by the front gate, and the group of seven began to pray over the property. They walked to the far end by the back gate, where each took a turn hammering one of the gold spikes into the ground. Then, on their way out, at the front gate they nailed down the other gold spike, declaring, "This is the Lord's property, to be used for his purposes. We proclaim in faith he will arrange for it to come into our hands, no matter what obstacles the devil may raise."

Not long afterward, the Golls received a call from their real estate contacts. The owners had just put the property back on the market. Needing a quick sale, they had not only lowered the price substantially but added five acres. The next day this bargain would hit the public computer listings, and the agents expected a rush of offers. "Are you still interested?" came the question.

Over the past months the Lord had miraculously provided some funds for the planned purchase. With the reduced sale price the Golls quickly arranged a deal with the sellers. The family closed escrow and moved to their secluded acreage in May 2000.

That fall, eighteen months to the week after Jim heard God's voice about the "hunters," fresh violence broke out in Israel. On September 28 Ariel Sharon, then Israel's opposition party leader and a lightning rod for Arab enmity, made a highly publicized appearance at the Temple Mount in Jerusalem, site of the Al Aqsa mosque. His visit sparked rioting that led within days to several deaths and hundreds of injuries. Soon an extended new Palestinian uprising mushroomed throughout the West Bank and Gaza Strip.

As Jim followed the news over the coming months, he observed attacks against Jews not only in Israel but in several nations across the world, with evidence of rising anti-Semitism. He prayed fervently and mobilized many others to intercede that God would extend a window of mercy as long as possible to allow Jews, particularly in the "land of the north," to find protection before the gathering storm clouds of persecution burst forth in fury.

Then, on the morning of September 11, 2001, the audible voice of God came to Jim again. Shortly before eight o'clock, as he sat in a steam room in his new home in Franklin, Tennessee, his ear heard quiet words: "The hunters have just been released." The voice, almost a whisper, seemed to want to share a secret.

What's happening? Jim wondered, a knot of dread twisting in his stomach. He left the bath and switched on the small television in his bedroom. His eyes widened as scenes of the burning World Trade Center in New York City filled the screen. Then on the live telecast he witnessed the second hijacked jet slam into the WTC tower.

As newscasters speculated about terrorist instigators, Jim felt in his gut an immediate conviction that—no matter what other issues the terrorists had against America—on one key level the attacks represented an assault against the Jewish people. As Israel's closest ally, the United States offers a huge target to enemies of that nation. Moreover, New York City is the world's largest Jewish city, with an estimated two million Jews in the greater metropolitan area. In light of this, Jim reflected on how Zechariah 2:8 calls Israel the apple of God's eye, and pondered, *Isn't it interesting that New York City is nicknamed The Big Apple?*

The Lord's whisper in his ear that morning, expanded over the next two months through other supernatural events, gave Jim a framework for interpreting the terrorist attacks and subsequent developments as part of the devil's larger, age-old scheme to destroy God's historic covenant people. In particular, he saw the urgency of prayer and action, and the promise of God's supernatural care and provision for Jews fleeing persecution.

In praying for the Jewish people, especially in Russia and the northern regions, Jim recognizes the dynamic relationship between prophecy and intercession. Almost all prophetic revelation of future events comes with one or more conditions, even if unexpressed. God's message through Jonah for the city of Nineveh stated, "Forty more days and Nineveh will be overturned" (Jon 3:4). Why was Nineveh still standing forty days later? Verses 5-10 explain how the inhabitants believed the divine declaration and responded with repentance, fasting, and prayer for mercy. The Lord then withheld the planned destruction because the people met the condition that was unspoken but in his heart all along.

The timing revealed in God's words to Jim did match specific events in the natural realm. Yet Jim continues to pray for restraint of "the hunters" to the extent possible for as long as God might allow. The Lord's first desire is to use "fishers," who want only good for the Jewish people, to woo them to their divine destiny and warn them of impending danger. If some fail to heed, God will then allow malicious "hunters" to target them, for the purpose of driving a remnant to seek him. Jim believes that as the Jews return to the land of their forebears from lands where they have faced persecution, they will awaken spiritually to the God of the Bible and return to him who remains faithful to his word and fulfills his promises.

To this end Jim has worked to muster intercession and acts of mercy toward Jewish people throughout the world. Others who carry a similar concern have joined in a United Prayer Coalition using a monthly rotation of thirty-one daily Scripture prayers specifically for Israel, America, and youth. Ministries supporting this effort include Lydia Fellowship, End-Time Handmaidens and Servants, Aglow International, Concerts of Prayer International, Intercessors for America, Campus Crusade for Christ, Promise Keepers, Derek Prince Ministries, the U.S. Prayer Center, and dozens of others.

In addition to prayer, what Jim believes is the largest humanitarian aid project in the history of the church was inaugurated during the summer of 2002 in conjunction with the Israel Relief Fund, for which Jim serves as one of the national directors. The M/V *Spirit of Grace,* an enormous cargo ship, will bring its load of food and supplies to the residents of Israel, both Jews and Arabs. Organizers hope in this way to build a bridge for all people to come to the knowledge of God's love through the Messiah.

As the Lord gives Jim ongoing supernatural revelation of his purposes for Israel, Jim continues to wrestle in intercession against the spiritual forces of evil that oppose God's will. Our prayers, Jim contends, can thwart the devil's plans for destruction and release God's mercy and power in signs and wonders, causing Jews and Gentiles alike to recognize him and receive his Son as Savior and Lord.

SEVEN

Victory Over Death and Dying

"WHY SHOULD ANY of you consider it incredible that God raises the dead?" (Acts 26:8).

Resurrection from the dead seems to be the gold standard for signs and wonders. If God can raise the dead, the thinking goes, he can do anything. Yet what makes one kind of miracle any more difficult for almighty God than another? The perceived degree of impossibility should not cause us to place this wonder in a higher category than others.

Terminology may present a stumbling block. Apart from the resurrection of Christ, many prefer to reserve the term "resurrection" for the resurrection bodies we will receive at the end of the age, when the dead are raised to stand before God's throne for final judgment, when at last "death has been swallowed up in victory" (1 Cor 15:54). According to this semantic scheme, a soul's temporary return to an earthly body would be better termed "resuscitation," no matter how long the body has been dead.

In the Western world, dramatic and irrefutable resuscitations remain rare. In many cases a person loses all vital signs for only a matter of minutes. Even if medical personnel are present to document a body as "clinically dead" (no pulse or respiration; fixed, dilated pupils), rescue workers may not yet have abandoned attempts to restore these functions. By contrast, stories from other regions and as nearby as Mexico, often well verified, may feature bodies dead for many hours or even days. Sometimes the decomposing corpse has begun to stink. In one widely reported account from Nigeria, documented on video by international evangelist Reinhard Bonnke, doctors issued a death certificate for pastor Daniel Ekechukwu following fatal injuries in a November 2001 auto accident. A mortician injected his body with a chemical solution in preparation for embalming. Yet Daniel, already stiffening with rigor mortis, revived two days later with no signs of his injuries.

Why don't we see more of such miracles? We will take a closer look at the role of faith and related issues in the final chapter. Beyond this, we can only speculate. Perhaps not many people, particularly in North America, actually die "before their time." We know little about the extent of Satan's ability to cut lives short against God's will. Even the most apparently untimely deaths may have some purpose hidden in God's omniscience.

A mindset that resuscitation happens rarely, or never, conditions us to look for alternative explanations, even more than with other signs and wonders. With good reason, many choose to exercise caution in the use of terms like "raised from the dead." We need not overstate the case if God "merely" brought someone back from the brink of death. Yet the latter constitutes a miracle in itself, especially if the person's body retains few scars from its ordeal. We dishonor God when we fail to praise him appropriately for wonders of all kinds because we want to see only the most sensational.

With that in mind, give God glory as you read these few samples of the numerous "North American-style" resuscitations taking place today. Maybe someday soon, as the Holy Spirit sets the stage for revival, we will see in our midst more demonstrations of the kinds of dead-raisings that even the most hard-core skeptics would have trouble explaining away.

Amid Death and Dying, God Speaks

The Harkness family was tired. Westside Church, their home congregation in Hemet, California, had hosted a prophetic conference over the past four days, inviting people from the surrounding community, some thirty miles southeast of Riverside. The family felt as though they had been living at the church most of the week. Yet Sue, for whatever reason, felt an urge from the Lord that everyone should return for the final meeting, on Sunday evening, March 4, 2001.

For Sue Harkness, a thirty-five-year-old wife and mother of three, the conference's guest speakers had already ministered to her family in profound ways. Her husband, Robert, age forty-four, had received a prophetic word from the Lord through Ed Lixey on Thursday, the first day of the conference. Then Ed had given another prophecy to both Sue and Rob on Saturday.

As Sue entered the sanctuary that Sunday evening, the fresh memory of the prophetic words gave her renewed encouragement. The divine messages spoke of abundant blessing and provision for the family. Rob had lost his job the previous November, and finances remained tight. Yet the Lord now promised that Rob would make double Sue's salary as a part-time instructional aide. Furthermore, his word for Rob included revelation of a new direction unfolding: "There's a natural circumstance getting ready to take place in your life that's totally going to turn your life around...."

During the service, people gave "popcorn testimonies," standing one after another to share what God was doing. Rob told how the Spirit had filled him earlier in the conference and touched him deeply. "In fact," he said, "I wish the Holy Spirit wasn't grabbing so hard on my chest, because it's beginning to hurt."

The congregation shared Holy Communion, passing the elements down the rows. In the quiet atmosphere, twelve-year-old Jessica commented to her mother how the air conditioning sounded like falling rain. Ten-year-old Andeanna sat nearby, while C.J., age seven, slept in his mother's lap. Sue thanked the Lord for how well her children had taken to Rob since their marriage two years before.

Just then, about a quarter to eight, she noticed her husband, to her right, leaning precariously back and away from her. As a former certified nursing assistant, Sue recognized that Rob was having a seizure. She pulled him up just as others began to realize something was desperately wrong.

Quickly people moved chairs and laid Rob on the floor. While trained in cardiopulmonary resuscitation, Sue felt stunned and immobile at the scene before her. She could only watch while someone gave Rob mouth-to-mouth resuscitation and two deacons with CPR training pounded on her husband's sternum, to no avail.

Someone called 911, and within minutes paramedics from the Hemet Fire Department and Valley Ambulance Service continued the fight over Rob's lifeless body. Four times they tried to restore his heartbeat, only to lose it again.

A couple of Sue's friends took her children to the lobby to spare them from witnessing more trauma. Another lady came over and said, "Suzie, Rob is having a nice talk with Jesus right now. Don't worry."

Her words birthed unusual faith in Sue's heart. God filled her with a sense of calm she had never felt before. Despite the hopeless situation in front of her, somehow Sue knew Rob was going to be OK.

After perhaps ten minutes in the sanctuary, paramedics abandoned their emergency efforts and hustled Rob to the ambulance, where they would continue attempts to revive him en route to the hospital. Netah Kruse, a deacon's wife, rode with Sue and the children as she drove home to get insurance cards. By God's grace, the Harknesses had extended Rob's health insurance after his job loss through a government policy for retired Navy personnel.

In the car Sue reassured her anxious children, who had seen Rob's pallid and lifeless body, by reminding them of the recent prophetic words. "God wouldn't have promised such a wonderful future if he was going to allow Rob to die," she said.

Netah stayed with the children while Sue made a beeline the few miles to Hemet Valley Hospital. After she arrived and dealt with the paperwork, a doctor in the Emergency Department met her. The E.D. personnel seemed to feel that something extraordinary had just happened. Not until later, however, did Sue learn more details about Rob's ambulance ride. When the paramedics had lost his pulse again, they had lost hope. They had expected the body they were delivering to go straight to the morgue. Yet just before the ambulance turned onto hospital property, Rob's pulse had begun on its own.

The E.D. doctor, Rakesh Gupta, told Sue her husband was getting a CT scan. He also said, "You know, Rob is a one-in-a-million patient." He explained how rarely they saw someone in full cardiac arrest receive CPR within three minutes and get to the hospital in under an hour—still alive. As a consequence, Rob qualified to receive a "clot-buster" shot to help restore circulation in his blocked arteries. Sue authorized this injection, effective only if given within an hour of a heart attack.

Soon friends from Westside Church began arriving, including Pastor Paul Ethington and his wife, Bonnie. They told Sue what had taken place after she left the service. The congregation had gone into intense intercession for Rob. Soon a corporate sense had arisen that the Lord wanted them to affirm his desire and intention to restore Rob to life. They had moved from petition to authoritative declaration of God's power over death, proclaiming Rob's miraculous resuscitation.

Within a few minutes, Pastor Paul recounted, the congregation had received assurance from the Lord that Rob was alive and would be all right. "We were so convinced of this," he explained, "we concluded the Communion service about twenty minutes later with a time of rejoicing that our prayers had already been answered," without yet hearing any reports about Rob's condition.

Later Pastor Paul and Sue made the connection: Just when the group at church had begun to declare God's miracle over Rob, his heart had started beating again on its own, after the ambulance crew had given up on him.

When Sue finally rejoined Rob, she was shocked to see blood everywhere—streaming from his nose and being suctioned from his mouth. "What's happened?" she asked the attendants.

They told her that during the ambulance crew's attempts to revive Rob's heart, they had tried inserting a nasogastric tube through Rob's nose but had accidentally nicked an artery. Then the clot-buster shot to clear his blood vessels had intensified the hemorrhaging. For the next twelve hours an attendant would pinch off Rob's nose to staunch the bleeding.

Sue also saw that the doctors had inserted a tracheostomy tube in Rob's throat so a respirator machine could breathe for him. Tubes and wires sprouted in all directions from her husband's comatose body, but Sue remained supernaturally calm. God's peace that passes understanding, as well as Sue's familiarity with medical equipment and procedures, kept her from the panic that might have overwhelmed many others.

Sometime after midnight, a bed opened up in the Intensive Care Unit. When Sue saw Rob again after the transfer, he still looked gray, but the heart monitor showed a steady pulse.

To the amazement of most friends and relatives, Sue's calm faith remained firm over the next two days, despite little change in Rob's condition. Then early Wednesday morning, she had a dream. She saw Rob sitting in God's lap. The Lord was so big that Rob looked about the size of an eighteen-month-old baby. Rob leaned on God's giant arm, his face aglow with peace and contentment.

Sue spoke with her heavenly Father. "You know, Lord, you promised us all kinds of incredible things on Saturday, and that can't happen if you keep Rob there. We're going to need him." God looked at Sue with kind eyes, and his response made her smile as she sensed his love. When she woke, the memory of this dream kept her spirit steadfast.

At the hospital on Wednesday morning, Rob's color and condition showed significant improvement. His vital signs strengthened. He began to move in response to touch. By noon he started fighting the respirator, and nurses took out his tracheostomy tube. That afternoon he was breathing on his own, eyes fluttering open, in and out of consciousness.

Sue stayed close by as Rob began to speak. "I had the craziest dream," he mumbled. "I dreamed I was taken out of the church in an ambulance."

Sue smiled. "That was no dream, Handsome."

By evening, Rob's persistent progress made him more talkative. He told Sue he could not understand why hospital staff had confined him to his bed, since he was in the ICU to visit the other men and women receiving medical care.

"What are you talking about, Honey?" Sue asked.

"Well, I've been spending the day with the patients, helping them relax," Rob answered. "You know, I don't have a job, so I might as well do something."

He described the other folks being treated in the ICU, what they were experiencing, who had come calling, and details about their conditions over the past two-and-a-half days. With amazement, Sue recognized the accuracy of his facts, although everything had taken place while Rob lay comatose. Moreover, the other beds, situated around the perimeter of the nurses' station with walls between them, stood outside his view.

Rob told about conversing with a woman on the other side of the ward, and how he had tried to calm her worries. He described her husband, her granddaughter, and the Mylar balloons in her room. Sue knew just the woman he meant, and confirmed his information after she spoke with the woman's husband later in the ICU waiting room. The husband shared with Sue that he had just about given up hope for his wife and had considered taking her off life support. She woke up within twenty-four hours of when Rob did.

By Friday Rob was sitting in a chair, telling tales of his military days. Late that night he was transferred to St. Bernardine Medical Center in San Bernardino for an angioplasty on Saturday to ream out his arteries. He came through in great shape. By Monday he was home.

Over the coming weeks Rob and Sue learned more about the

extent of their miracle. Rob's brain had gone without oxygen for thirty-two minutes, from the time of his seizure until the clot-buster shot had kicked in. The neurologist, Dr. Abdul Jaffer, could not understand how his tests showed no evidence of brain damage.

Rob's primary-care physician, Dr. Abid Hussein, who had last seen him in the Emergency Department, could hardly believe his eyes when Rob came for a visit two weeks after his discharge. "I am looking at a miracle," he declared. "You are not supposed to be here—you're supposed to be dead."

His cardiologist, Dr. Anil Rastogi, also expressed amazement at Rob's rapid progress and soon gave him a clean bill of health. By July Rob started a new job doing custodial work for the Hemet Unified School District, Sue's employer—with a salary scale double what Sue makes, and full benefits. The man who was supposed to be dead is now exerting himself physically even more than before.

"There's a natural circumstance getting ready to take place in your life that's totally going to turn your life around...." At the time of this prophetic word, Rob and Sue could never have imagined how true it would prove. And the Lord's promises continue to unfold as the Harknesses share their miracle testimony, to the glory of God.

A Battle for One Soul's Salvation

"The Lord told me something about your meeting tomorrow, Mike," Adriana Medina said to her husband. "It's good news and bad news...."

Mike Medina knew that when God spoke to his wife, he had better pay attention. The two had served in ministry together since just after their marriage in 1985. In their mid-twenties and fresh out of Bible school, where they met, the couple began missions work in 1986 in Chile, Adriana's native country. During the fourteen months they served alongside the pastor at her home church in Santiago, they saw the congregation grow from about 70 people to 350. Moreover, this initial missions experience gave them their first exposure to the supernatural, including a vital and practical deliverance ministry.

Over the years the Lord developed Adriana's prophetic gift. Mike grew to trust when she was hearing from God. So he prepared to listen closely to the word she received about his meeting the next morning, Friday, October 20, 2000.

This gathering, billed as a "Funders Forum," linked foundations and corporate donors with nonprofit organizations seeking grants. Since the family's return from South America on furlough in August, their two daughters, Leeann and Jennifer, had been attending a Christian academy in Dallas, Texas. Mike had volunteered to help the pastor of the school's sponsoring church in efforts to raise funds for an athletic field. At the Funders Forum they hoped to get guidelines on applying for donations from various philanthropic groups.

Now Adriana had a prophetic word about the meeting. "I hear the Lord saying you're not going to get any money for the school out of your contacts tomorrow. But someone at the meeting is going to be saved!"

This news got Mike's juices flowing. He enjoyed few things better than leading people to Jesus Christ. His and Adriana's ministry in South America had centered on planting new churches and equipping other church planters. After Chile they had worked for three and a half years in Argentina, then found a special calling in Uruguay, the least evangelized country in the Americas. Uruguay presented a formidable spiritual battleground. The society was steeped in witchcraft cults and New Age influence with its capital, Montevideo, hosting the new headquarters of Rev. Sun Myung Moon's Unification Church. The Medinas relished the challenge and witnessed new levels of God's supernatural power.

They had returned for their current furlough with plans that included the establishment of a Bible school in Uruguay to prepare ministers for the spiritual harvest they believed was coming. Both Mike and Adriana had received training and credentials through Christ for the Nations, a missionary organization and Bible institute based in Dallas, and made that area the home base for their stay in the United States.

When Pastor Greg picked up Mike the next morning for the Funders Forum in downtown Dallas, Mike did not have the heart to tell him nothing would come of their efforts that day to get money for the school. He did relate the other part of the word: "Adriana says God told her somebody at the meeting is going to be saved today." The men rejoiced and prayed together during the drive.

As the crowd of about 120 mingled over coffee before the meeting, Mike rode high on a wave of anticipation. *Is this the one, Lord?* he asked silently each time he introduced himself. Yet nobody captured his attention spiritually.

The forum started, and Mike took a seat at the right end of the third row of chairs. He turned his focus to the panel of speakers sitting behind tables at the front of the room. The woman convening the forum sat next to the tabletop podium, with two more people to her right. Two others sat to the left of the podium, closer to Mike. The emcee introduced the presenters one by one, beginning at the far right end of the panel.

As the first speaker stood, Mike prayed for her. *Lord, let this be the person you will save today! Lift any cloud of darkness over her mind and shine the light of your truth. Bring her to the foot of the cross.*

Mike sensed nothing special as the first speaker sat down and the next one rose. He prayed similarly throughout that man's presentation. Pastor Greg beside him scribbled notes about grant deadlines, filing requirements, and the like, but Mike concentrated on clearing the heavenly airways for the one God had destined for salvation.

When the second man finished, the emcee introduced the next speaker. This woman stood and Mike interceded for her as before. *In Jesus' name I come against any spirit of darkness blinding her mind from seeing the light of Christ.*

Only about ten minutes into her presentation the woman, probably in her mid-forties, caught Mike's gaze from the third row. Her eyes locked on his. She paused, stammered, and looked away. She tried to resume her talk, but halted again. Leaning over slightly, she muttered, "I'm not feeling too well."

The woman's eyes bulged, and she grabbed the back of her chair to try to sit down. In a moment her limp body collapsed to the floor.

The emcee leaped to her feet and came to kneel next to the speaker as a buzz of concern rose throughout the audience.

"Does anybody here know CPR?" the emcee shouted. "She's not breathing! There's no heartbeat!" Her voice filled with desperation. "Can somebody please do something?"

Throughout the hall people whipped out cell phones, dialing 911. Yet no one knew CPR. As minutes passed, a murmur arose from the small group huddled around the body. "She's dead! She's dead!"

In his spirit Mike discerned a counter-assault by demonic forces that preferred this woman dead rather than saved. He stood and walked behind the table.

"I'm a pastor," he said. "May I pray for her?"

The emcee cried, "Please! Someone do something!"

With the lifeless form now beginning to turn cold and purple, Mike knelt and laid his right hand on the woman's head, raising his left in intercession. Quietly he prayed aloud, rebuking a spirit of death in the name of Jesus and by the power of the Holy Spirit. He called the spirit of life to return and fill her body.

Perhaps ten minutes passed while others continued futile attempts to discern a pulse. Suddenly the woman's motionless eyes jerked and she gasped for breath. As her eyelids fluttered and she continued to suck in air, the cry went up: "Oh my God, she's alive! She's alive!"

The woman looked at Mike. "Thank you for praying," she

told him. "I—I don't remember what you said, but I could hear your voice." She went on, "Please give me your card. I want to call you tonight and thank you."

Before Mike could dig out a card for her, he sensed the Holy Spirit instructing him, *Have her sit up.* Obediently, he asked the woman, "Would you like to sit up now?"

The revived speaker said yes. Yet the emcee, her voice still heavy with fear, interjected, "No! Don't touch her until the paramedics get here! They're on their way!"

When Mike heard the Spirit repeat his instruction, he smiled at the emcee and responded gently, "I think it will be OK if we let her sit up."

Just as she did, the woman began to cough and gag. Because of his experience ministering deliverance, Mike knew what was happening. He spotted a wastebasket with a plastic liner behind the table and asked calmly, "Could someone please pass me that wastebasket?"

Placing the container under her chin, Mike continued to pray in Jesus' name and told the speaker, "Whatever is in there, just let it go." He heard others nearby speculating that the woman had choked on her breakfast. When she vomited a noxious white glob, however, Mike knew it wasn't bacon and eggs or a Danish roll. The demons that wanted to kill her had surrendered under the saving power of God.

Just then the paramedics arrived. Mike stepped aside. Checking the woman's vital signs, the emergency team found everything normal. They recommended she come to the hospital for tests and monitoring, but she told them, "I feel fine!" After making her sign a release form, they left without her.

Several people advised the speaker to go home and rest. She gathered her things and walked to the door. As a precaution, someone volunteered to drive her car for her, with someone else following to bring the driver back to the meeting hall. On her way out Mike gave her his card.

The Funders Forum continued, but Mike heard little of the

last speaker's presentation. Now he could not wait to get home.

That night the woman phoned him. After her brush with death, her receptivity to the gospel skyrocketed. Mike led her in a prayer of faith in Jesus. Their joy overflowed.

Because she lived on a different side of the Dallas/Fort Worth Metroplex, he could not reasonably invite her to come to church with his family, but he recommended she find a Bible-believing congregation in her neighborhood. She said she would.

Mike did not stay in contact with the woman, and can only trust that she has become involved at a church home where she can grow in her faith. Yet he still feels the Lord's pleasure as he recalls that October morning. His wife's word of knowledge persuaded him to set aside the day's agenda, his time wasted for its original purpose, in order to see one soul saved from death— both physical and spiritual.

A Vision of Life in the Face of Death

Sallye Burton's heart sank when she got the news. Doctors had diagnosed her sister, Carolyn Combs, with multiple myeloma, a rare form of cancer affecting the blood and immune system. *Lord, why does she have to suffer so much?* Sallye wondered.

Carolyn had already endured a bout with another form of the dread disease. Back in October 1974, cervical cancer had led to a hysterectomy. That surgery had eliminated the malignancy, giving Carolyn a long span of good health afterward. Sallye also thanked God that in the midst of this affliction her sister had called asking her to pray with her for the first time since Sallye had come back to the Lord.

The sisters, Carolyn four years older, and their younger brother had been raised in the church, but each one had drifted away at different times. When Sallye had recommitted her life to Christ and become involved in the early 1970s in Women's Aglow, an international Christian women's ministry network, her family had rejected her decision. Carolyn, in particular, had closed her ears to any kind of religious talk. Yet after she developed cervical cancer she had called Sallye, asking for prayer.

Despite this opening, Carolyn had not taken any more steps toward the Lord. Sallye had seen some danger areas in her sister's life that might allow a foothold for demonic activity. For instance, Carolyn had always had a fascination with Halloween, one of her favorite holidays.

In her ongoing prayers Sallye had engaged in a spiritual battle for her sister's soul. Then, in October 1995, Carolyn had almost died of pancreatitis. As her sister struggled for her life at Hendricks County Hospital in Danville, Indiana, Sallye had driven about an hour and a half north from her home in Bloomington to see her. Her sister had looked terrible, but for the first time Carolyn had allowed Sallye to pray for her in person, and Carolyn had recovered from the brink of death.

The pancreatitis had returned with another even more virulent attack a year later. Carolyn had never quite regained full strength after that bout, becoming seriously anemic. Now, in April 1997, doctors had found cancer in her blood and bones.

Sallye wrestled with this news as her heart went out to her sister. She learned that treatments for multiple myeloma could be brutal, as malignant plasma cells accumulated in the bone marrow, weakening the bones. Yet she kept faith that God could heal Carolyn, and continued to pray. For five years Sallye had been involved with the United States Spiritual Warfare Network, now known as the U.S. Strategic Prayer Network. The fifty-something intercessor had spent many hours bringing individual and corporate concerns before the Lord.

At this same time, Sallye's husband, Robert, was struggling with life-threatening health issues, including advanced diabetes and kidney disease. On November 30, 1997, he graduated to his heavenly home. Sallye pressed closer to God to find her strength in him.

During 1998, Carolyn underwent numerous chemotherapy treatments, with cocktails of powerful chemicals aimed at poisoning the cancer cells. Her condition took several ups and downs over the months.

On the twenty-sixth of October, Sallye hosted a family get-together for the birthday of one of her five sons. In the midst of the celebration that Monday evening, her phone rang. It was one of Carolyn's two daughters, calling from the hospital.

"Aunt Sallye, I'm afraid you'd better get up here," Celana said. "Mom's in Critical Care and not doing well at all. She really wants you to come."

After relaying the dire news, Sallye linked hands with her sons, a daughter-in-law, and two granddaughters, and they prayed urgently. Sallye threw a few things into a suitcase, apologized for leaving the dinner party, and rushed to her car. As soon as she could safely do so, she used her cell phone to call an intercessor and get some other people praying.

Many thoughts filled her mind as she drove. With no assurance that her sister knew the Lord, Sallye felt a heavy burden to pray for God to save her before she died. Memories replayed of occasions in years past when God had given Sallye a similar prayer charge.

Back in the mid-1970s, she had gotten news that a young friend who had strayed from the Lord was hemorrhaging from the liver and not expected to live. Sallye had not been able to reach anyone else to join in intercession, so she had grabbed her own children's hands and asked them to agree with her in prayer that this woman would not pass into eternity unsaved. At her funeral, Sallye had learned from her friend's husband that fifteen minutes before she died, she had come out of her coma and asked her brother-in-law, a minister, to come pray with her.

Then in 1981 an unsaved uncle in Florida had lain dying of cancer. Sallye had called a prayer partner to intercede in agreement for him to turn to Christ. During the family's death watch, her uncle had regained consciousness and had a vision of Jesus. When a Methodist minister came, her uncle had prayed with him for salvation. Moreover, he had left the hospital and lived another six months before going to be with the Lord.

As these scenes crossed her mind's eye during the drive to Hendricks County Hospital, the ring of her cell phone interrupted Sallye's thoughts. One of her intercessors was calling back. The year before, Sallye had agreed to become the Indiana state coordinator for the U.S. Spiritual Warfare Network. Because of this strategic leadership position, she had organized a "prayer shield" of intercessors to cover her and her ministry. Her cell call earlier had mobilized many from this group to go to their knees.

The woman on the phone said she and several prayer warriors from Terre Haute had gathered right away to lift up Sallye and her sister. "Do you want to pray together now?" she asked.

Sallye readily agreed, holding the cell phone in one hand while she drove with the other. As they prayed, in the midst of everything competing for her attention, Sallye had an open-eyed vision.

She saw her sister lying in her hospital bed with the Holy Spirit hovering over her. She watched as the Spirit blew into Carolyn's face, breathing on her. Sallye recalled the verse from Genesis 2:7, when the Lord God "breathed into [Adam's] nostrils the breath of life." Then the Spirit quickened to her mind the passage in Ezekiel 37 when the Lord commanded Ezekiel to prophesy life and breath to the valley of dry bones.

Sallye described what she had seen to her friend on the phone. "The Holy Spirit is telling me, 'Prophesy life!'"

By now, nearly 10:00 P.M., she was approaching the hospital. Once inside, she got directions to Carolyn's bed in the Critical Care Unit.

Just as she neared the room, her brother-in-law, Gene, and two nieces, Celana and Ceann, came bursting out into the hallway. They saw Sallye and cried, "She's gone! She's gone!"

Her nieces sobbed inconsolably. Yet Sallye felt as though the Lord had put her inside a bubble of peace. She had never experienced anything like it. She heard her family's cries and words, but they did not penetrate her.

With their mom now dead, the young women were too distraught to linger. "We've got to go home; we can't stay here," one said. Sallye hugged and released them.

Gene gave Sallye permission to enter the room. There she found Carolyn lying lifeless, with no vital signs. Her years of dealing with her late husband's illnesses had taught Sallye how to read medical equipment. Carolyn's heart monitor could not have told the tale more clearly: The glowing flat line moved straight across the screen.

No one else was in the room at the moment. In obedience to the Holy Spirit's prompting, Sallye put anointing oil onto her fingers and began to prophesy life over her sister. She placed one hand on Carolyn's forehead and held her hand with the other. Praying aloud, she took authority over a spirit of death and released the spirit of life, declaring to her sister, "The Holy Spirit is breathing life into you."

A nurse came in and out, but Sallye remained at her sister's bedside, doing as the Lord had told her. Later her brother-in-law returned with a doctor who had been called in at that hour, not Carolyn's regular physician. The monitors continued to register lifelessness, and Gene told Dr. DeWeese that since his wife had not wanted heroic measures, it might be time to pull her off the machines.

The doctor was unwilling to take that step just yet. He placed some orders, and three nurses along with a technician came to work on the body. They did not shock Carolyn's heart with a defibrillator, but they gave her an injection and put something into her intravenous solution.

Sallye did not pay much attention to them as she prayed aloud and pursued focus on her assignment from the Lord. She asked one nurse, "Am I in the way?"

The nurse leaned over and whispered into her ear, "Honey, you just keep doing what you are doing."

The Spirit gave Sallye verses to pray, including Ezekiel 18:32:

"For I take no pleasure in the death of anyone, declares the Sovereign Lord. Repent and live!" According to this Scripture, she commanded her sister, "Turn and live! I forbid you to die, in the name of Jesus Christ!"

Sallye kept prophesying life over Carolyn, with little sense of time passing. It must have been about midnight when Pastor John Irwin from Hope Presbyterian Church in Plainfield, Carolyn's hometown near Indianapolis, joined her at Carolyn's bedside. He introduced himself. To Sallye's amazement, she learned that her sister and brother-in-law had been attending church for some months, not just in the hit-and-miss pattern of the past. In response to Sallye's question, Pastor John expressed his belief that Carolyn had recently come to saving faith. Sallye's heart leaped with joy.

For the next couple of hours the pastor stood on the other side of Carolyn's bed and prayed with Sallye. During this time the nurses seemed to work more intently as changes began appearing on the monitors. Sallye, so focused on prayer, did not realize just when it happened, but at some point Carolyn's heart started to beat again. One by one her vital signs returned and her organs revived. By about two o'clock in the morning, Sallye felt released from her prayer assignment to prophesy life. It was done.

Gene Combs, still at the hospital, had been resting in a waiting room across the hall most of this time. When he got the news that Carolyn now lived and breathed, his face went white.

Gene and Sallye spent the rest of the night at the hospital, checking on Carolyn periodically. In the morning Sallye spoke with her sister, who had no memory of the previous night. Dr. DeWeese, however, knew everything that had taken place and said frankly, "This is a miracle."

The staff soon moved Carolyn to a regular private room, and she did not receive any special medication or lifesaving measures during the rest of her stay until her discharge the next week.

During a follow-up visit about two months later, doctors ran various tests and detected no sign of multiple myeloma. They declared Carolyn cancer-free. They also found, however, that the chemotherapy had elevated her toxin levels. Amyloidosis, a disease caused by malfunctioning bone marrow, complicated matters.

Yet over the coming year Carolyn gained weight and strength and seemed to be doing well. Sallye rejoiced to see her sister grow in the Lord. Then in early October 1999 Carolyn began experiencing nausea. She continued to get around and take care of her family until later that month, when doctors discovered blood clots. They scheduled surgery, but before it could take place Carolyn passed into eternity on October 23, her spiritual destiny secured.

Knowing that her sister was at rest in God's arms, Sallye did not cry over her death. She only wished she could have spent more time with her as a sister in the Lord.

Because of Carolyn's experience, her family became increasingly open to prayer and the influence of the Spirit. Younger daughter Ceann met Jesus in a powerful way in the fall of 2001 and was baptized the next summer.

As Sallye reflects on these events, she concludes, "We Christians have to get hold of the fact that hell is a real place. And God never intended for any person to go there. He says he does not want anyone to perish," she notes, citing 2 Peter 3:9.

Although at the time of Carolyn's crisis Sallye did not know her sister was already saved, her desperation at the condition of her sister's soul prompted fervent, anointed prayer that brought her from death to life. Perhaps an urgent concern about the finality of death for the lost is precisely what God may use from time to time to intervene supernaturally in situations where death might not be so final, after all.

"I Can't Even Die Right!"
Saturday, January 22, 2000, marked Sandra Woody's sixty-second birthday. Instead of a celebration, however, the day

brought an ambulance rushing her to the hospital in the throes of death.

Her thirty-seven-year-old daughter, DeLaena Dixon, had planned to visit her mother that morning. She and her husband, Gary, drove a couple of miles across Conway, Arkansas, bringing gifts along with their children, fifteen-year-old daughter Sebrina and son Andrew, not quite thirteen.

When they pulled up in front of the apartment complex where her mother lived, DeLaena saw an ambulance. Her heartbeat quickened, but DeLaena refused to consider the worst. *In a retirement facility like this,* she reasoned, *it could be anyone.*

Several somber-faced folks milled around the lobby. One elderly lady approached DeLaena and asked, "Are you Mrs. Woody's kin?"

DeLaena almost dropped the wrapped package in her hands. "Yes, what's wrong?" she cried.

The woman just patted DeLaena and said, "Go on upstairs. It will be OK."

The door to her mother's apartment stood open as DeLaena and her family approached. Inside, a team of medical personnel scurried about. They asked DeLaena to wait in the hallway, then brought out her mom on a gurney and whisked her to the ambulance.

Only the nurse who had found Sandra Woody gave DeLaena any information. When Mrs. Woody did not answer the door that morning for her daily checkup, the nurse called 911 and her door was forced open. The paramedics detected no pulse, and assumed she had suffered a heart attack. When CPR did not help, they used a defibrillator to jump-start her heartbeat again.

"Go on to the hospital and meet us there," a paramedic told DeLaena before the ambulance sped off.

DeLaena shook her head as if to loose the nightmare from her consciousness. *This can't be happening—not again!* Only a week before, her mother had come home from the hospital after a brush with death. That nightmare had begun on the day after Christmas.

As her husband drove the family to Conway Regional Hospital, DeLaena's mind replayed the events of recent weeks. The flu bug had hit hard that year, but her mom was especially vulnerable because of her eleven-year history of lung disease. In addition to Chronic Obstructive Pulmonary Disease (COPD), commonly known as emphysema, Sandra Woody had diabetes, and used a portable oxygen unit. When she became ill that holiday season, her family took her to the Emergency Department at Conway Regional, where physicians immediately moved her to the Intensive Care Unit, her lungs full of fluid.

At first, doctors suggested that her condition did not pose a serious threat. Once they drained her lungs, they moved her to a regular room and monitored her condition before preparing to discharge her. Yet early on Friday, December 31, Mrs. Woody developed a bad coughing spell. She coughed up an alarming amount of blood from her lungs, and soon returned to the ICU, where she was placed on a ventilator.

Dr. Gary Bowman, the family's primary-care physician and a Christian, suggested to DeLaena that she contact any family members who might want to see her mother, because her life hung in the balance.

DeLaena had already activated the prayer chain at their church, a Full Gospel congregation called House of Prayer. She thought and prayed for some time, however, before contacting a half-brother named Butch. She and Butch, seven years older, had only sporadic communication. Scarred by a troubled background, Butch was difficult for DeLaena to understand. Furthermore, his history of unpredictable violence left DeLaena and their mother a bit afraid of him.

When he arrived, however, DeLaena sensed something different about him. He seemed calmer and kinder than she remembered from any time since their childhood. *Could God already be at work in his life?* she wondered.

Over the next week, as their mother lay in the ICU, DeLaena learned that Butch had been attending church the past few months with the friend who had brought him to the hospital. One afternoon a discussion in the hospital cafeteria turned toward faith and salvation. Butch and his friend, along with DeLaena and a good friend, joined hands to pray, and Butch asked God to make him his child.

When they told their mother that Butch had given his heart to Jesus, her condition improved markedly. The next day doctors weaned her off the ventilator, and a day later she transferred out of the ICU. By that weekend she left the hospital.

Home health care nurses and other aides helped Sandra Woody monitor her blood sugar and take eighteen kinds of medication. For a few days she seemed to regain strength. By Wednesday, however, she became dehydrated and developed a severe case of thrush. Dr. Bowman and her heart specialist, Dr. Donald Steely, were concerned but wanted to give her time to recover from her ordeal.

Late Friday, the night before her mother's birthday, DeLaena got another call from the home health care nurse. Her mom's thrush made it painful for her to eat, aggravating her dehydration. In addition, her blood sugar level kept dropping. DeLaena forced her mom to take some instant mashed potatoes and orange juice, then tucked her into bed in anticipation of a birthday celebration the next day.

Instead, the family found themselves back in the Emergency Department at Conway Regional Hospital.

Doctors determined Mrs. Woody had suffered a massive heart attack. Moreover, kidney failure had caused her serum potassium level to spike, as her renal system no longer filtered her blood adequately. The potatoes and orange juice of the previous night, both loaded with potassium, had helped send her serum level skyrocketing to 9.7 milliequivalents per liter (normal is about 3.5 to 5.5). DeLaena's husband, Gary, learned that no one had ever recorded potassium levels that high and survived.

Dr. Steely, the cardiologist, was already on call at the hospital and met the Dixons in Emergency before transferring DeLaena's mother to the ICU. Just outside Mrs. Woody's cubicle, he asked DeLaena about her mother's wishes regarding life-support measures. "Would she want to be put on the ventilator again?" he asked.

Before DeLaena could answer, they heard a voice from the cubicle call out firmly, "No!" The same reply came when Dr. Steely asked about life-prolonging treatments, given that Mrs. Woody's kidneys had shut down and she risked another heart attack. "No!"

DeLaena and the doctor, another fellow believer, gave thanks that Sandra Woody could make and express this decision herself. He wrote on her chart, "DNR—Do Not Resuscitate."

Once again, Gary and DeLaena activated the church's prayer chain and started calling relatives and friends. This time, however, the pall of death hung in the air. Mrs. Woody began slipping from consciousness. Loved ones came to the hospital prepared to say good-bye.

Several hours later that Saturday, DeLaena learned that her mom had received dialysis treatment. Dr. Steely explained that dialysis often is not considered extraordinary life support, so the team had not asked permission. Yet, in fact, the blood filtering procedure did not work as hoped, and her mother's potassium level began rising again. When faced with the prospect that—if she survived at all—she would need regular dialysis the rest of her life, Gary, DeLaena, and Butch made a decision based on their mom's wish to forgo life-prolonging measures: No more dialysis.

DeLaena took up a vigil at her mother's side. For days she never left the hospital. Friends and family brought her food and comfort as they came to pray or cry with her, sing to Mrs. Woody, or just hold her hand in silence. DeLaena used a public restroom to wash up until hospital personnel moved her mother upstairs to a regular room with a private bath.

As renal failure took its toll, Sandra Woody's death was merely a matter of time. Without extraordinary measures, she received only standard "comfort care," including intravenous nutrients, a bladder catheter, and a mask for oxygen, since the usual nose cannula caused a rash. Doctors stopped administering morphine after a day, but with her mom's semi-comatose state DeLaena thought she appeared still drugged. Mostly she lay unresponsive; occasionally she moved, glanced around, or mumbled incoherently.

Assurance that her mom would be with the Lord after her death helped DeLaena release her to God and his will. DeLaena's faith had grown strong since she had given her life to Jesus at age twenty-three, after a turbulent childhood as a victim of sexual abuse. Because of all the sins and traumas from which God had delivered her, she felt his heart of mercy toward the lost and hurting. Now DeLaena serves with her church's outreach department as director of evangelistic drama productions.

On Wednesday, January 26, about three o'clock in the afternoon, DeLaena and Gary sat in the hospital room with Zee Matson, a friend of her mother, and DeLaena's best friend, Kerri Tindall. A nurse came in and out, checking monitors. Suddenly Sandra Woody turned her head to the left, eyes open wide, and spoke to her daughter with perfect clarity.

"DeLaena, do you know that turquoise dress of mine with the pleats?"

A moment of shock passed before DeLaena could reply. "Uh, yes, Mom; I know which one you're talking about." She shot a questioning glance at Kerri, who nodded with a calm look that said to her, *This is it; your mom's about to go.*

Mrs. Woody continued on about the dress. "Well, that's the one I want to be buried in."

"All right, Mom," DeLaena answered. Despite her wonder at what was happening, she felt no fear—only a supernatural peace.

"Get a pen and paper," her mother instructed her. "I want you to write this stuff down." For the next twenty minutes or so, Sandra Woody planned her own funeral and gave directions for disposition of her belongings. Talking quickly and lucidly, she identified item after item and the person to whom she wanted each to go. She explained to Gary the details of her financial arrangements and insurance policies.

"Now, I want the service at House of Prayer, of course," Mrs. Woody went on. Naming the church worship leaders, she said, "Tell Steve and Christy what songs I want sung." She mentioned two or three favorites, including "Ain't No Grave Gonna Hold This Body Down."

"Understand," she continued, "I don't want no sad singing and no slow walking. I want a celebration!"

"Yes, Ma'am," her daughter replied.

She then turned to DeLaena's husband. "Gary, you take care of my baby. Watch over Andrew and 'Brina. And make sure Butch is OK, now that God's got ahold of him." She took her daughter and son-in-law's hands and expressed her love for them, bringing tears to DeLaena's eyes.

Then Mrs. Woody lay back, pressed her right hand onto her left shoulder and crossed her left hand onto her right shoulder. She smiled and closed her eyes. "OK, I'm going to be with Jesus now!"

Her amazed visitors stood around her bed, praying and praising and asking the Lord to send angels quickly to come get her. DeLaena felt a strong peace and presence of the Holy Spirit.

After a few minutes, however, DeLaena noticed her mom's right eyelid crack open. She looked up at her daughter. "Honey?" she asked. "I thought I was already gone!"

"No, Mom, you're not gone yet," DeLaena told her.

Her mother shut her eyes again, hands still positioned on her shoulders. A while later she piped up, "Where's the light? I don't see the light!" She glanced around. "And that's got to be the ugliest green wallpaper I've ever seen!"

For quite some time Mrs. Woody rambled on, resting intermittently. She expressed her disappointment at not sighting the expected walls of jasper and streets of gold. Sometimes she seemed to be talking to the Lord.

As the sun set outside the window, Sandra Woody's visitors sensed heavenly joy as well as humor as they watched God's hand at work. Her good friend Sandy Ray came calling that evening. When Mrs. Woody saw her, she reached for her hand. "What's going on, Sandy?" she asked with a tear in her eye. "I can't even die right! Why didn't I go?"

"Well, you know, Sandra," her friend replied, "maybe this just isn't your time. God knows what he's doing."

By the next morning, when a nurse came to take another blood test of her oxygen saturation, the level was not just normal but beyond—101 percent. DeLaena and Kerri watched as the hospital staff unhooked the oxygen mask. Their pastor's wife was also visiting then, and Ricki Distin noticed that urine collecting in a bag from the catheter now ran clear, with none of the blood Mrs. Woody had passed in previous days. Both lungs and kidneys now functioned properly.

Throughout that Thursday, God restored each of Sandra Woody's organs, one by one. Test after test convinced the doctors to disconnect all her tubes. Dr. Bowman, the primary-care physician, told her, "Miss Sandra, nothing's gonna get you down!" Dr. Steely, the cardiologist, noted in her chart that he had witnessed a miracle. The doctors knew nothing they did could have saved her; they gave all credit to God and rejoiced along with the family.

That weekend Sandra Woody was discharged to a rehabilitation hospital in Little Rock, thirty miles south of Conway. For the next two weeks there, she became known as "the woman who prays." Other patients and staff wanted to meet and receive prayer from this miracle woman, and many received a touch from God.

DeLaena's mother now lives at home, without nursing care. She keeps a portable oxygen unit in her apartment in case of emergency, but has needed it only once. DeLaena still marvels as she recalls her mom's previous eleven years of daily oxygen use.

For many months when she met people at church and elsewhere, DeLaena's mother introduced herself this way: "Hi, I'm Sandra Woody; God raised me from the dead!" Both she and DeLaena have promised the Lord they will take every opportunity to testify about God's resurrection power, giving him all the glory.

And one day in the future, when God alone decides her time has come, Sandra Woody will be fully prepared to "die right." After all, she has been down that road before. Next time the destination won't include green wallpaper.

EIGHT

Rain and Fire: The Cost of Revival

WHEN JESUS HEALED a man born blind, a major scandal erupted. The apostle John took the entire ninth chapter of his Gospel to report it. The Pharisees fumed because the healing occurred on a Sabbath day; they labeled Jesus a sinner for working wonders when work was outlawed. The unprecedented miracle ("Nobody has ever heard of opening the eyes of a man born blind," Jn 9:32) so consternated the man's neighbors that they could not decide if he was the same guy they had seen begging for so many years.

The disciples likely marveled that Jesus had healed him at all. Their initial question to their Master about the blind man revealed a theological misunderstanding. Jesus answered their inquiry in a most unexpected way:

> As he went along, he saw a man blind from birth. His disciples asked him, "Rabbi, who sinned, this man or his parents, that he was born blind?"
>
> "Neither this man nor his parents sinned," said Jesus, "but this happened so that the work of God might be displayed in his life. As long as it is day, we must do the work of him who sent me. Night is coming, when no one can work. While I am in the world, I am the light of the world."
>
> Having said this, he spit on the ground, made some mud with the saliva, and put it on the man's eyes. "Go," he told him, "wash in the Pool of Siloam" (this word means Sent). So the man went and washed, and came home seeing.
>
> JOHN 9:1–7

Jesus' answer indicates that God uses some human suffering for the purpose of magnifying his glory when he brings relief through supernatural works. Jesus also reveals an urgency to do as much of this work of God as possible before it is too late.

In chapter 1, we noted that Jesus did nothing on his own authority but only what he saw his Father doing (see Jn 5:19). One might reasonably conclude that the Father is active for the purpose of signs and wonders often enough that his Son saw the need to minister diligently without pause until his days on earth ended.

Can we assume the same today? Does God want to release his power much more frequently than we imagine, waiting in many instances for our participation in the delivery of his blessing to the needy? If so, an urgency arises to fulfill God's purposes in the brief span of life he has given us, because every day the end of the age draws nearer.

Responding to Signs and Wonders

As God gears up for the great worldwide revival expected to usher in the return of Christ, signs and wonders pointing people to him will take place more often. If, by definition, miracles are unusual events provoking awe and wonder, what happens when they begin occurring more frequently? Regularity will not make them any less a demonstration of God's power. Yet will we become apathetic and stop responding with praise and glory to God for each manifestation? If so, the Lord may eventually withdraw his hand.

Many believe a response of gratitude that honors God for even the smallest evidence of his supernatural touch is an essential condition for experiencing greater and more frequent wonders. No matter how often miracles may occur, they will always remain subject to God's sovereignty. We cannot order them up like room service. We may become less surprised to see the Lord exercise his power in our circumstances, but we should never become less grateful.

Depending on the purpose of a particular miracle, another response—besides praise and thankfulness—might prove even more crucial. In Matthew 11:20-24 Jesus issued this warning:

> Then Jesus began to denounce the cities in which most of his miracles had been performed, because they did not repent. "Woe to you, Korazin! Woe to you, Bethsaida! If the miracles that were performed in you had been performed in Tyre and Sidon, they would have repented long ago in sackcloth and ashes. But I tell you, it will be more bearable for Tyre and Sidon on the day of judgment than for you. And you, Capernaum, will you be lifted up to the skies? No, you will go down to the depths. If the miracles that were performed in you had been performed in Sodom, it would have remained to this day. But I tell you that it will be more bearable for Sodom on the day of judgment than for you."

Jesus suggests that when the sovereign God performs miracles in our midst, we have a responsibility to turn to him in repentance and rededication of our lives to him. When a holy God chooses to move among us, we cannot remain impassive to his glory or callous about our sin. As famously sinful as the people of Sodom were, Jesus says they will get off easier than those who did not respond appropriately to the signs and wonders they witnessed.

The Role of Faith

Many passages in Scripture indicate a link between faith and the manifestation of supernatural signs. Likewise, unbelief plays a role in blocking the release of God's power. The people of

Nazareth had heard about Jesus' miracles. Yet when he returned to his hometown to teach them in person, they took offense at him. Mark 6:5-6 says, "He could not do any miracles there, except lay his hands on a few sick people and heal them. And he was amazed at their lack of faith."

As we saw previously, Jesus pointed to repentance as an appropriate response to signs and wonders. Since the Bible brands doubt and unbelief as sin (note, for instance, Hebrews 3:12), our lack of faith becomes an issue for us to confess and renounce.

People today believe that doctors and medicine can heal, or even that the body can heal itself. No one hesitates to accept reports of such cures. Yet when the claim is made that God has healed, we want to see X rays, videotapes, and medical reports. Collecting evidence in honest inquiry or as documentation of a miracle is valuable and needed; requiring proof because of a heart of skepticism reflects the kind of unbelief the Bible condemns.

Why is it often so hard for Christians who believe God *can* heal to have faith that he *will* and *does*? If we cannot take our faith from the cognitive to the experiential, how much faith do we really have? What holds us back from believing God more?

Western worldview presents one stumbling block to faith. In the United States our scientific rationalism, while not without worth, often blinds our eyes from seeing what God is doing in the supernatural realm, or even acknowledging that such a realm exists. Only the Holy Spirit can provide a more accurate view of reality in all its aspects. The more we press in to God, the more he will expand our perspective to see the scope of his nature and ways.

In cultures like that of the United States, repentance for unbelief may be appropriate not only as individuals but also on the church, community, and national levels. Confessing our lack of faith may break a stronghold that has constrained a greater move of God and hindered his people from doing his will, including ministering in signs and wonders. A widespread dismantling of this demonically inspired mindset would change the spiritual atmosphere in North America.

Praying in faith does not mean denying contrary evidence. Many healings, in particular, occur over time rather than instantly. Some miracles require alignment of circumstances to God's will before he can release his power. When we do not see manifestation of God's work in our timetable, we can go wrong in two ways: concluding the Lord does not want to answer, or placing faith in our faith itself by never praying about something more than once in fear of expressing unbelief. Either way, our intercession stops.

Real faith is persistent in seeking God's will (see Lk 11:9 and Heb 11:6, among many such passages). Effective, faith-filled intercession rests on confidence about what the Lord wills in a given situation. Once we have heard from him, we can pray tenaciously until we see fulfillment of his promise.

The Role of Motivation

In addition to the importance of praise, gratitude, repentance, and faith in the outpouring of the Holy Spirit, our motivation for pursuing signs and wonders is crucial to whether God will respond. Especially as we minister to others, our desire to bless people, to meet their needs with compassion, to draw them closer to Jesus, and to glorify God's name will please him and position us to see him act in power. If, in contrast, we are motivated by a selfish craving for the sensational, God knows better than to answer such prayers. He also knows when deeply rooted skepticism has created an unholy zeal to seek out signs for the purpose of refuting them and justifying unbelief.

We harden our hearts when the Lord reveals his majesty in the supernatural events we demand and we respond with continued doubt, upping the ante for ever more spectacular demonstrations before we think our quest for proof will be satisfied. Jesus recognized this pursuit as a wasted effort:

"Then some of the Pharisees and teachers of the law said to him, 'Teacher, we want to see a miraculous sign from you.'

"He answered, 'A wicked and adulterous generation asks for a miraculous sign! But none will be given it except the sign of the prophet Jonah'" (Mt 12:38-39).

Examining the motivation of our hearts will prove vital as we desire and pray for a powerful spiritual outpouring in our nation. The depth and sincerity of our prayers and repentance, with fasting as God leads us, will help determine the depth of revival God sends.

Our understanding and experience of the awesome beauty of God's nature will also increase our motivation to see his glory revealed. James Goll, who shared a story in chapter 6, wrote in his March 2002 "Visioncast," a monthly e-mail communiqué from Ministry to the Nations, about a prophetic vision he received. In it he saw a lame man sitting outside an arched gateway labeled "BEAUTIFUL" (recalling the account in Acts 3:1-10). Inside the gate Jim felt the weight of a glowing substance like semi-liquid gold, heavy with the glory and presence of God.

Jim realized that the lame man signifies the millions still sitting outside the kingdom of God who need someone who has seen the beauty of the Lord to touch them with his presence and goodness and show them the way inside. Beholding God's beauty fills us with love for him, which, in turn, inspires us with his love for others and a desire to convey his loving presence in power. "I am convinced," Jim says, "that a new level of signs and wonders will be released as we pass through the Gate called Beautiful and turn around and release what has just captured us."

The Role of Humility

Another important component of the coming revival is humility. One of the biggest hindrances to the move of God's Spirit in the United States has been our independence and self-reliance. When we perceive few needs we cannot meet in our own self-sufficiency, we leave little room for divine providence. Believers living in poorer nations may see more miracles in many cases because they need them more, and recognize their dependence on almighty God to act on their behalf. He receives more glory when the earthly vessels he uses come nearly empty of their own resources.

Our nation's abundance does not have to hold us back from seeing the flow of the Lord's power. However, we must abandon our trust in our assets and lay them all before God, who provided them and still holds claim to them. America will experience spiritual transformation when we grasp the truth of Jesus' words, "Apart from me you can do nothing" (Jn 15:5).

Humility extends to recognizing the spiritual debt America owes to Christians in other nations. We who have given the gospel to the world in generations past now need to humble ourselves and receive from our brothers and sisters around the globe who are praying for us. As they intercede for awakening and revival in the world's most powerful nation, they know from experience that the Lord may send spiritual outpouring on the heels of persecution and suffering.

We need their prayers and their example of what it means when God's Spirit comes in power and purifies with fire. In many countries the spiritual maturity of the church, the expression of God's kingdom, and the display of his glory in signs and wonders far surpass the norm in the United States. Believers from Africa, Asia, and South America have much to teach us about the practice of faith in their daily lives, their dedication to prayer, their sacrificial obedience, and their endurance of hardship and persecution. Some people have actually followed God's call to come to the United States as missionaries to our secular humanist culture.

Persecution and Revival

Rick Joyner, founder of MorningStar Ministries in Charlotte, North Carolina, writes in "A Time for Miracles," his Word for the Week from August 28, 2000, "Almost every miracle is the result of a desperate need. The greater the need, the greater the miracle.... It is at the point that we see our resources running out that we will experience the power of God."

God may be bringing us to our extremity in order that his glory might shine forth more clearly as our lives and society pass through his refining fire. Believers within the United States will need strong faith, endurance, and obedience, relying on God and living in close communication with him, to withstand the hardships of assault from our secular culture as well as from non-Christian religious cultures. As we show ourselves faithful in response to each challenge, the Lord will give us more challenges, more opportunities to respond in faith, and more demonstrations of his supernatural power in the face of urgent need.

Throughout history and in today's world, Christians have learned that persecution and revival often go hand in hand. Rick Joyner concludes, "We are about to see great miracles because [God] is going to allow us to come into places where we are going to need them."

The signs and wonders we witness in America today are most likely the early rains of a greater outpouring of God's Spirit in power than we have ever experienced. The rain is coming with the fire of his purity. If we respond in humility and obedience, the outbreaks all over the country will expand and multiply until whole communities and regions catch flame and our society is transformed.

God is answering the prayers of Christians from other nations who know how much we need a move of the Holy Spirit in the United States. Intercessors around the world are waiting to see revival poured out in America. It will come. It is happening now. By his grace, the most influential nation on the planet will soon be exporting a higher quality spiritual life along with ministry in the supernatural, instead of a culture of rationalism, unbelief, and self-sufficiency. When America comes into the fullness of God's destiny, his exercise of power in and through us will change the world and prepare it for the return of Christ.

As we give thanks and praise to God for the signs, wonders, and miracles he is working in our midst today, let us pray that he receives all the glory he deserves through the sacrificial devotion of our lives to the advance of his kingdom, no matter what it costs us.

Come, Lord Jesus!

Index